THE
VICTOR
WITHIN

Christmas 2000

Dear Matt,

Merry Christmas + hope you enjoy
the book.

Love

Colin, Colleen, Bradley + Lauren
xxx

THE VICTOR WITHIN

An extraordinary story of optimism, tenacity & sheer determination

By Victor Vermeulen & Jonathan Ancer

Foreword by Christopher Reeve

TENACITY

First published 2000 by Tenacity Publications
PO Box 92043, Norwood 2117, South Africa
Tel: 011 640-6722
Fax: 011 640-4016

ISBN 0-620-26485-3

Typeset & Reproduction: Pointset, Dover Street, Randburg
Printed & bound by CTP Book Printers (Pty) Ltd., Caxton Street, Parow 7500
Cover design: Peter Arabatzis
Front cover photograph by Anne Brest
Editor: Mary Ancer

To Mom and Dad
for their love and dedication
and for always encouraging me to be
the very best I could be.

To Maggie Keebine for being my second mom.

Contents

Victor's
Mission Statement

I will live each day in courage and gratitude, showing a deep sense of appreciation to people like my mom, who has encouraged my progress and development and supported my efforts to be the very best that I can be. I will operate by the values of integrity and continuously strive to fulfil the commitments I have made to the people around me and to myself. I will never take life for granted and I will endeavour to live each day to the full, remaining aware that my strength of character and optimism can make an essential difference in the lives of others. My sense of self-worth is constantly reinforced by my own personal triumphs and victories. I will not allow myself to become bogged down in self-pity or anger, because I recognise that life is too precious to waste. Regardless of the fact that my physical body is confined to a wheelchair, I will encourage my spirit to soar, so that I can help those in need through my ability to motivate and inspire.

Foreword

Most of us go through life spending very little time, if any, contemplating how we and our loved ones would be affected by a catastrophic illness or injury. Or, if we do think about having to face MS, Parkinson's, diabetes, a stroke or a spinal cord injury we imagine (or at least I did), that our one life on this planet would have been ruined, not only because of the loss of normal activity but our perceived inability to endure.

Victor's book and the compelling mission statement for his life proves otherwise. He shows us that we have two simple choices in the face of adversity: to give in to loss, or to reach new heights by discovering the power within. Victor has made the courageous choice and has much to teach us.

Christopher Reeve
September 2000

Thanks & Acknowledgments

First and foremost, I would like to express my heartfelt thanks to all my family and friends for their help and encouragement over the past eight years.

I am tremendously grateful to everyone who worked for and supported "The Victor Vermeulen Fund" especially Di Featherstone, Sharon Slater, Bill Fenner and Mike Tyler and to all the guys from Gauteng Cricket and the "Robbie Burns Foundation" (David Rawlinson, Willy McClure, Hugh Moffat, Dennis Stewart and John Dewar).

A sincere thank you also, to all the South African companies who have helped make my life a little easier especially MTN (Steve Tredoux, Kenda and Mel), Renault (Mannie Capazorio, Phonnie and Lee) and National Data Systems (Jack Horton and Simon O'Hagan).

I am particularly indebted to Norman Adami of SAB who gave a resounding "Yes" when we approached him to support this project and to the team who put it together - Jon-Jon (the best collaborator a man could get) and his wife Mary, Anne Brest, Valerie Diesel, Peter Arabatzis, David Williams, Marietjie Coetzee and Linda Coetzee.

An enormous thank you too, to Christopher Reeve who took the time and trouble to watch the video tapes of me in action on the speaker circuit, read an advanced copy and write the foreword.

And, last but certainly not least, to Juin Cassie for making it all happen!

Victor Vermeulen
September 2000

Introduction and acknowledgements

I always thought writing a book would be novel (if you'll excuse the pun), but I never realised how extraordinary that experience could be. I was very fortunate that the subject of the book was motivational speaker extraordinaire Victor Vermeulen. Whenever I was overwhelmed by deadlines or depressed about the state of South African cricket, Vic would encourage me to hang in there. He never gave me any pep talks either. He motivated me by simple example - his courage, dignity and determination. Vic was a fantastic cricket player who was well on his way to representing his country before he was rendered a quadriplegic. Vic has chosen words as his new calling and is now a motivational speaker without parallel.

As soon as Vic and I met I knew we were going to get along. Every day for a month I camped at the Vermeulens to interview Vic, his mom Isabella and his second mom Maggie. In between Vic's demanding schedule on the motivational speaking circuit, a movie called 28 Days and a visit to the hospital, Vic told me about his life. He travelled back in time, reliving terrible moments like the day his father was killed and the day of his accident. He also told me stories that were so funny that I wept.

In the evenings, I listened to the recordings and made notes about what to ask him the following day. Once the tapes were transcribed I organised them into chapters.

The book slips in and out of first and third person narratives. I chose this style because I felt that first person style might falsely suggest that Vic is boasting when he talks about his cricket success or feels sorry for himself when he talks about his disability. This is certainly not the case and if there was any suggestion that it is then I would be negligent in my duties as a writer. (Incidentally, Vic was reluctant to talk about his sporting achievements and I had to rely on newspaper clippings and anecdotes from those with whom he played for information about that chapter.)

Vic, Isabella and Maggie welcomed me into their family and gave me endless cups of coffee and plates of lunch. Gentle, tough and generous people; nothing was too much trouble. Sorry, Maggie, but I still don't eat peas.

Writing this was not a simple project and I am indebted to a number of people for their assistance and guidance. To Moira Killian for transcribing 22 hours of taped conversation into 463 pages; to Dr LJ 'Vic' du Plessis for checking all the medical information, and to Adam Bacher, Andrew Kramer, Jenny Michaeli, Natie King, and Sheila and Big Vic for taking time to chat to me about their friend.

Thanks are also due to mom and dad for checking my grammar, and for your unbounded and unconditional love and your belief in me. To Judith, Andrew, Ruth, Charles and Romi for your support and falafels. To John and Sue, my parents-in law, thank you for carefully reading the manuscript, giving sensible advice and for your never-ending support. Special thanks to Samuel, Benjamin and Sabelo for being there.

Finally, to Mary who polished, pruned and guided me through every single step of this book. We did this together. The best thing I ever did was to marry this very gifted and capable editor. You are my hero.

This experience really changed my life. I hope that by meeting Vic in the pages of this book it will change yours.

Jonathan Ancer

CHAPTER 1

5 November 1992

"I dare you," she said.

It was just before midnight on Guy Fawkes Night, November 5. The night was warm; in the distance I could hear fireworks exploding and howling dogs. Five of us were standing by the swimming pool, enjoying what was left of the annual Wanderers Cricket Club braai.

It was the end of a tumultuous year. I was 19 years old and had been picked to represent Transvaal as a professional cricketer; I'd just returned from a tour of England with the squad. It was also the year my father was murdered.

"I'll bet you R100 you won't," she said.

We'd eaten some steak, drunk some beer and because it was a warm and muggy evening, two mates and I decided to skinny dip. We were standing around, ragging each other, when a couple of girls arrived. My friends chickened out of swimming in the buff. I was still keen, but it seemed unfair.

"Well, if you two aren't going to skinny dip then why should I be the idiot who does?"

And then it came.

"I dare you," one of the girls said. "I'll bet you R100 you won't."

Nobody dares me. I stripped, ran down the embankment and dived. It was a bomb dive: I was trying to be funny, trying to make a big splash.

As I came down I realised I'd dived too deep, but it was too late. I couldn't stop myself. I grabbed at the Kreepy-Krauly but it didn't slow me down. It takes only four kilograms of pressure to break a neck. I'm 6'3", and with all that momentum I didn't stand a chance.

As I hit my head on the bottom of the pool, I knew I'd screwed up big time. It was as if a light had been switched off.

I floated to the top of the water, face down. I couldn't move.

I thought: "God, if I die here, please take me up to heaven to be with my dad. But God, if you can, let me stay alive because I know how much mom is hurting since dad died." I knew that if I died my mom would go to pieces. "Please let me be with my mom," I prayed.

I was trying to breathe, swallowing water, beginning to drown. My ears were above the surface and I could hear my friends laughing. There I was, buck naked, floating face-down in the pool. Vic, the joker, was obviously just fooling about again. But I couldn't move.

The strange thing is that I remained calm, almost resigned. I knew panicking wasn't going to help, and maybe I also realised that now - for once - it was all out of my control.

At nineteen my philosophy was, "Life's a lag". Like all young people, I was enjoying my life. Nothing could happen to me. I was invincible. I could do anything. The cake was in front of me and all I had to do was take the cream off the top. I was young, I was good at what I did, I had good friends and I was having a good time.

The evening before the braai both my mom and Maggie, our domestic worker, urged me to stay at home. My mom had bought me a double bed that day: my old single bed was now too cramped for my height. I was really pleased with the new bed. I'd carried it up the stairs myself, on my back, and had a quick snooze on it in the afternoon. I didn't know that was the last time I'd use it.

"Stay at home, Vic," my mom said. "Watch a video and enjoy your new bed early." But I had to go to the cricket braai.

In the afternoon my cousin phoned and invited me to join him and some mates for a drink. I told him I had to go to the cricket braai. On my way to the braai, I bumped into two girls I knew and they

2

asked me to join them at the pub. Not even the girls could persuade me.

"No," I told them, "I've got to get to this cricket braai."

The joke was going on for too long. One of the girls started screaming. I'd been floating face-down for more than two minutes, and she suddenly realised what was happening.

My friends all jumped into the pool. Wet, naked and immobile, they pulled me out. As they laid me face-up on the paving the first thing I did was to yell, "Cover me!" In the midst of it all, I was worried about what the girls would think. Typical male, thinking with the other head: you know what shock and cold can do to a guy's anatomy.

They covered me, shouting, "Vic, Vic are you all right?" I didn't answer. I knew I was paralysed. All that my friends knew was that I'd been drowning, and they had to get the water out of my lungs.

Without supporting my neck, they rolled me over onto my left side. These boys knew First Aid: they knew rolling me was the way to get the water out. What they didn't know was that my neck was broken.

As they moved me my spinal cord, already seriously damaged, sustained more injury. My neck was just flopping about. I'm not saying that if they had supported my neck I would have walked, but I might have had a better chance. I might have got something back, maybe even movement in an arm. But there we all were, young, panicking, late at night and faced with something devastating and unexpected: in their position I probably would have done exactly the same.

I later learned that for neck injuries in swimming pools, there's a procedure called a 'log-roll'; two or three people hold the patient, supporting his neck and keeping his spine straight, and then roll him carefully.

As they rolled me I vomited up the water from my left lung. In a way, they did good: if that lung had collapsed I would have been in serious trouble. I wasn't rolled to my right side and so my right lung collapsed.

While we were waiting for the paramedics my friends started to argue. They were stressed; they couldn't deal with what had happened. Within five minutes we'd gone from having a good time, enjoying life, to a serious, life-threatening situation. I was the life and soul of the party, and now I couldn't move and might not survive.

The tension didn't ease off when help arrived. Like most quadriplegics, my reflexes are still intact. One of the paramedics gave me a reflex examination: when I responded positively, he assumed I was faking my paralysis. He asked me straight out if I always played such stupid pranks at parties.

My friends couldn't deal with this. They were panicking. All they wanted was for the nightmare to be over, for the paramedics to put me in the ambulance and start caring for me. Some punches were nearly exchanged.

Finally, we managed to convince the paramedics that something serious was going on. They put a collar around my neck and stretchered me to the ambulance.

As we drove off a paramedic asked which hospital I wanted to go to. "Joburg General," I told him: a state hospital. Despite the trauma I had the presence of mind to realise that after my father's murder, my mother and I no longer had medical aid. I knew we couldn't afford a private clinic.

As we were rushing through the traffic, the ambulance siren whirring, I could feel myself fading away. I passed out.

CHAPTER 2

Thrown in the Deep End

It is 5 a.m. on a frosty Johannesburg winter morning, nearly 8 years after the accident, when I first meet Victor Vermeulen. He's lying on the hospital bed at his home in Randpark Ridge, and as I walk through the door he gives me a big grin. Automatically I extend my hand in greeting.

"Can't shake hands, Jon," Vic reminds me with a mischievous smile.

Isabella, his mother, and Maggie, the domestic who has been with the family almost all of his life, have just finished the morning routine. They've turned him, given him a sponge bath, shaved him, brushed his teeth, inserted a catheter, dressed him in a dark blue suit and combed his hair. He looks handsome, immaculately groomed. I am to discover that Vic always looks this way. His reddish-brown hair is stylishly cut, his face clean-shaven with freckled, boyish good looks. But I can't describe Victor's body language; this body is now mute.

"Everything is still there, but I can't move it," Vic explains. "It's like the cord of a telephone that's been cut. You can try and phone all day, but you won't get through. It's the same with me. You can pick up my arm and put it down. There is nothing wrong with the limb or the muscle. But when my mind tells my leg or arm to move, the message doesn't get through. The wire's been cut."

"How are you feeling?" I ask awkwardly.

"Feeling? Me? No, no I'm paralysed; I'm still not feeling." He grins again.

Vic is expert at using his sense of humour to put people at ease

5

about his condition. Through his optimistic, courageous and often very funny philosophy Victor, a man who can only move his neck and shoulders, has become a sought-after motivational speaker. His message - value what you've got, not what you haven't got - has become a source of inspiration to many. The accident broke Victor's neck; it did not break his spirit.

As he regained consciousness eight days after the accident, Vic found himself looking into the kind eyes of a hospital nurse. She was shaving him. It felt like heaven, and for a second he forgot about hitting his head at the bottom of the swimming pool. Then he felt the screws in his head and the tube in his throat; he saw pipes and drips and hospital walls. He realised that this could in fact be hell.

Isabella Vermeulen burst into tears when she heard her son was awake. Since the phone call eight days earlier, her life had been filled with anguish.

Isabella recalls: "At about a quarter to midnight, Vic phoned me. After his dad's murder he was always very worried about me. He wanted to sleep over at his friend's place, but needed to know I would be okay. I did wish he would come home because I was lonely in the house by myself. It had only been seven months since Tokkie's death. But Vic was nineteen. I said it was okay, I'd see him in the morning. I put the phone down, turned on my electric blanket and went to make a cup of Milo. I was thinking about Vic, about how good he was looking. He'd recently returned from a holiday in Greece; he was muscular and as brown as a berry. Then the phone rang again. "Now what?" I thought. It was Vic's friend Gavin. He told me Vic had been in a pool accident and was at the Johannesburg Hospital. I was alarmed, but not scared: Vic's been in scrapes all his life. I told Gavin I'd meet him at the hospital, but he insisted on coming to fetch me. I didn't understand. When Gavin arrived he seemed very upset. A pool accident? It couldn't be more serious than a broken arm. I started to feel confused.

"As I walked into the hospital I heard Vic's friends in the waiting room: they were crying. A nurse led me to my son. The sight of him, unconscious, his face bloated, reminded me of my husband's lifeless body stretched out on a hospital bed. The doctor told me there was only a four percent chance that Vic would survive.

"I went to wait with Vic's friends, and I started to babble. It must have been the panic. I talked about my husband; I talked about Vic and the mischief he got up to when he was young. Eventually a nurse led me to the trauma unit. Vic was lying on the bed, tubes and gadgets all over him. He really looked bad, but I wasn't going to give up. I'd lost my husband. I wasn't going to lose my son. If I had lost him I don't think I'd have had anything to live for."

Isabella began a week-long vigil at the hospital. Friends would bring her food, which she didn't eat. Vic was unconscious for eight days. She sat by his side, waiting. "By the sixth day I was at my wits end. The doctor said that even if Victor regained consciousness there was no telling how badly his brain had been damaged. Then a nurse suggested I talk to Vic. Maybe he would hear something. 'Vic,' I whispered, 'if you can hear me give me some sort of sign. Please son, do anything to show that you know it's me.' While I was talking he blew me two kisses. Just like that. I started crying, and the nurses started crying. Two days after that Vic woke up."

Victor started to gain strength in the hospital's trauma unit. After regaining consciousness he was wheeled into theatre for an eight-hour operation to reattach his head to his spine. The surgeon chipped bone off Victor's hip and squeezed it between the damaged vertebrae in the spinal column to fuse his skull back on. The operation was successful.

"I came out of the anaesthetic to the pulling and prodding of one of the nurses. She wanted to take me to be X-rayed. I was in pain and I wasn't in the mood. 'Leave me,' I mouthed soundlessly. She marched off, muttering that I needed a psychologist. A psychologist was duly sent to see me. Afterwards he told my mom, 'Victor doesn't need me. There's nothing wrong with him psychologically.'"

But Victor wasn't in such good physical shape. He couldn't eat solids, could not talk and he breathed only with the help of a respirator. A pipe, known as a tracheostomy, or trachey, is attached to the ventilator. The pipe is inserted into a hole in the throat. Frequently a thin catheter is inserted in the throat to suction out excess phlegm and mucous.

Morphine and pethidine cocktails took care of Victor's pain.

Not long after the operation, the doctor walked into the ward. He turned to Victor and without preamble he blurted: "Don't think you'll ever walk again. Don't think you'll ever breathe by yourself again. Because you won't." He then turned around and walked out again. Victor tried to talk, but the only sound that came out was little gasps.

That's when Victor realised how serious the situation actually was. "I knew I'd screwed up big time... big, big time. You can make mistakes in life and you can apologise, you can make up for what you've done, but when you break your neck there is no fixing it. There's no second chance. And there's no one to apologise to. From the start, I knew I had to get on with my life. I'm glad that I was the one responsible for the accident, because that made it easier for me to cope with the consequences. If somebody else was to blame, I think it might have taken me longer to come to terms with it all. And then there's my mom... I knew I wouldn't be able to get through it alone; knowing that my mom's love and support would be there made it easier."

Vic resolved to prove the doctor wrong. He may never walk again, but he was going to breathe on his own. "I was determined to get off the trachey. I wanted to breathe again when I chose to, not when a machine made me. It was so strange. Two weeks earlier I had thoughts of opening the batting for the South African cricket team. My ambitions were centred on hook shots, cover drives and late cuts. I would practice foot movements for hours and study ways of confronting reverse in-swingers, crafty flippers and furious bouncers. Now my main goal was simply to breathe.

"I realised that with the obstacles I faced, I needed to draw on every bit of my strength to get over them, one by one. It's victories - however small - that give us the will to persevere and to fight back."

Normal breathing is controlled by the diaphragm and the chest muscles working together. The chest muscles control deep breathing and other respiratory functions like coughing, while the diaphragm is responsible for shallow breathing. But they all work together: none of us could really say when we're breathing with the diaphragm and when we're breathing with the chest muscles.

The diaphragm is controlled by a nerve that sprouts from the spinal cord very high in the neck; the nerves for the intercostal chest muscles lower. Because Vic's injury was so severe, he had lost the use of his intercostal chest muscles, but he could still control his diaphragm. But breathing with the diaphragm alone is a difficult, tricky business. Vic had to train himself to breathe again. It would take a lot of time, a lot of practise, and a lot of perseverance.

"I kept trying to talk to my visitors; this helped my stomach go up and down, which trained my diaphragm. The more I tried to talk, the more I was actually just breathing without really knowing what I was doing. Then, bit by bit, I trained myself to breathe off the machine. At first, just five seconds on my own. Then 20 seconds. A minute. Three minutes. Five minutes. 20 minutes. An hour. The doctors inserted a long, thin needle in my foot, keeping it there to tap my blood. Three times a day they'd check the oxygen levels in my blood to ensure I was breathing properly.

"The first time I was fully off the trachey I lasted three or four days. Then I suddenly started gasping for air. The doctors checked my blood oxygen saturation level and things weren't looking good. The trachey hole in the throat heals very quickly, so they had to cut my throat again to reinsert the trachey. I had no anaesthetic, and my body can feel from the nipples up. It was like someone slashing my throat with a knife.

"I was on the machine for another month. I had to learn to breathe

9

again from scratch. Five seconds on my own. 20 seconds. A minute. Three minutes. Five minutes. 20 minutes. An hour.

"The second time off the trachey I breathed for myself for five days before I again started to gasp for air. They wanted to put the trachey back in, but I begged the nurse to give me another chance. I knew it would be incredibly difficult to learn to breathe again a third time. The nurse thought about it, and then came with a scapula to cut into my trachea. She didn't put the trachey back in; instead, she inserted a pipe to suction the mucous out of my lungs. I started to breathe a bit better. My lungs were cleared again four hours later, and I was still breathing. I haven't had to go on the trachey again."

Victor received first-rate medical care at the Johannesburg General Hospital. "The nurses were caring and did their utmost to look after me. On nights they weren't sure I'd survive they would let my mom stay with me. When my dad was shot four times by robbers he drove 16 kilometres on his own to get help, and died on his own in hospital. We didn't get to say goodbye. If it was going to happen to me, my mom and I wanted to have that opportunity. So on the bad nights she would sleep on two big chairs pushed together and the nurses would cover her with a blanket."

Attached to Victor's head when he was admitted to the hospital was a device known as halo traction; heavy weights hanging from his neck to pull it back into alignment. "The weights were attached to my head with screws - real screws, real hardware, screwed right into my skull - two in the front of my head and two in the back. The weights hung over the end of the bed and pulled my head backwards, my whole body arching off the bed. This for three months.

"Finally, the halo traction was taken off. When the force of the weight was removed the pain was excruciating. The doctor took the screws out with a screwdriver. People are usually anaesthetised for this procedure. But I was awake, and the doctor was trying to do it quickly, to minimise the pain. In his haste, he forgot to unscrew one at the back. So when he removed the halo traction, he ripped the screw straight out of my skull. I was in agony. The worst pain I've ever felt in my life. Breaking my neck wasn't even that painful."

At first, Vic was disoriented. Nineteen years old, in pain where he could feel and paralysed where he couldn't, the hospital kept Vic on morphine and pethidine painkillers.

"I loved it when it rained. I couldn't play cricket, and I was glad the rain was keeping my friends from playing as well.

"As I lay there on the hospital bed, I would focus on this little spot on the ceiling: this became my safety net, my cocoon. Each day I would line myself up to that spot. It would make me feel safe.

"One day, my mom and the doctor moved me, raising my bed a little so that I could see the view from a window looking out over Johannesburg. I got dizzy. I wasn't used to my body being raised, however slightly. I told them to put me down and to take me back to my little spot, to the place I felt comfortable.
The morphine would really confuse me. I thought the wall in front of me was the ceiling and the ceiling was the wall. I'd keep saying to my mom, 'Where are my feet? Are they on the ceiling?'"

Vic could only move his head and shoulders; everything below that was paralysed. When he had broken his neck, the spinal cord inside it was irreparably damaged.

The spinal cord is the information superhighway of the body's central nervous system, a column of nerves connecting the brain to the rest of the body. Like the Internet, it allows a two-way flow of information. The stomach, for example, can send signals to the brain that it is empty; the brain can then order the hand to pick up that burger and the jaws to take a big bite. Because of its importance, the spinal cord is protected within the spinal column, what you and I know as the spine or the backbone. This is in fact a series of bones called vertebrae, which extend from the skull down to just above the buttocks - 24 in total.

When the spinal column is broken and the cord within it damaged, some part of the body is paralysed. The higher the broken vertebrae are in the spine, the more severe the disability. Closest to the brain are seven cervical vertebrae - the neck bones. Within these are the nerves that process information to the neck, shoulders, arms, and hands. Film star Christopher Reeve, who broke his neck in a horse riding accident in 1995, fractured the second cervical vertebra (C2) - and so he's only able to move from the neck up and struggles to breathe on his own. Victor broke the third, fourth and fifth vertebrae in his neck (C3, C4, C5) which means he can move his head, neck and shoulders, but has lost essential body functions, like bladder and bowel control, sexual response, and any sensation or movement below his nipples. Only the heart and brain continue to function normally.

The result of spinal cord injury can never be predicted with absolute accuracy. When a person's neck or back is broken, the spinal cord becomes inflamed; the extent of actual damage can only be determined when this swelling goes down. At the hospital Victor met a man who, three months after being declared a quadriplegic with a C 3/4/5 break, walked out of the ward. It can take up to a few months for the swelling in this part of the body to go down. "When I first got to the hospital I was hoping I'd get something back. It was basically 'pray and wait'."

Victor wasn't the only one praying. Many people who'd read media reports about his accident and news of his progress were also praying. While in hospital he received tons of mail, letters of support, hope and admiration. Victor's bravery, his winner's attitude, was already an inspiration to many people.

Dear Victor
I am a cricket fanatic. I watch every game, ball for ball, and I can imagine what cricket must have meant for you. I was feeling sorry for myself because I've broken up with my boyfriend. Then I heard that you were in the hospital and you would never play cricket again and your bravery touched my heart.

12

Dear Victor
I only know you from your picture, but I was struck with your courageous and charming smile. You are in my prayers. I'm in my 70s and would be proud to call you "grandson". Bless you.

Dear Victor
It saddens me that a vibrant young man like you should have suffered such a severe accident, but I know you have the courage and perseverance to come out on top!

Dear Victor
I was distressed to hear of your bad luck. You have certainly had a load of misfortune land on your young shoulders. My heart goes out to you. It was good to hear that you are so positive. You are obviously not letting things get you down - good for you, Victor. May you develop talent and abilities that will fulfil your wishes to remain a useful member of society. I will think of you often.

Vic was surprised and touched by this groundswell of support. The people who wrote to him seemed to find him an inspiration, yet Vic himself drew encouragement from their letters. "I would lie in my hospital bed and hear these amazing messages of support from complete strangers. I wanted to answer every single letter, but with all that was happening, I never got the chance."

After that Vic decided to make the most of his hospital time, entertaining his friends. Because he'd been in the Transvaal cricket squad and cricket board officials had been in contact with the hospital, the hospital administration gave him celebrity status. Victor was allowed to receive visitors in the trauma unit.

"At first my speech was poor; people couldn't understand what I was saying. But my mom understood me. I'd talk to people and they would smile and nod and laugh. But I could tell that they had no idea what I was saying.

"Sometimes I'd say, 'You know, you're a real prick,' and the person would continue to nod and grin. My mom found this hilarious. Afterwards, we'd tell them what I'd said, and my friends would laugh and laugh.

"My mom quickly became one of the boys. Looking after me is a full-time job; she's with me nearly 24 hours each day. There is nothing I can hide from her. I didn't want to censor myself when my friends visited, so my mom soon got to know my naughty side."

Vic's stepsister Sheila remembers that her brother received so many visitors the hospital had to set aside a special waiting room just for them. "Sometimes even that room wasn't enough," recalls Sheila. "It would get full and people would have to wait in the corridors. Sometimes I would have to wait two hours, just to see him for ten minutes. We were only allowed to go and see him two at a time

"I remember one visit, when Vic had been in hospital for a while. I was used to him not being able to talk properly: he could only whisper at us. He asked me to come closer, gasping, "Come here, come here." He told me to put my ear to his mouth.

"I put my ear to his mouth, and in a completely normal voice he said: 'Hello sis.' He had learned to speak properly again. I looked at him for a second and then I burst into tears."

Sheila struggled to come to terms with the terrible thing that had happened to her little brother, the boy who was young enough to be her son.

"He was such a physical boy, so active. He always had something on the go. It was heartbreaking to see him just lying there, motionless.

"If I saw a youngster walking in the street, I cried. If I saw a youngster driving in a car I cried. If I saw a youngster dancing I cried. I was very angry. I was angry with God."

Andrew Kramer also struggled to understand the meaning behind his friend's accident. "The first time I saw Vic in hospital, I broke down. I'm not very religious, but afterwards I went to a Rabbi and asked him why bad things happen to good people.

"When I went back for my second visit, I was amazed at how cheerful Vic was, despite what had happened. I realised that this man is an inspiration. The loss he has had to come to terms with, the obstacles he had to face every single day: these were phenomenal. But he was determined, and he did it."

The nurses in the hospital helped raise Vic's spirits, with a little help from his old 'beat box' music system.

"I had the 'beat box' next to my bed with vibey music," Vic remembers. "Every morning after my bath the nurses would put it on, and we'd have a little party. I would bob my head and the nurses would dance around my bed. It was a great way to start the day. The nurses were super friendly, and it really made a difference. Flashing smiles and affectionate gestures all contributed to a better day. I needed better days. I didn't need people walking around with long faces, disgruntled with life, because life in my situation is hard enough as it is.

"I used to laugh all the time. I developed a friendship with a brilliant nurse called Nicole. Her husband had died of cancer, and because she had nursed him, she knew how to control pain. The other nurses would wait for the pain to arrive before injecting me with morphine, but Nicole would inject me before the first injection had worn off, so by the time it did wear off the new pain-killer would kick in. Nurses are only supposed to be with a patient for one or two days at a time so they don't become too emotionally involved, but Nicole would swap with the other nurses so she could look after me. It might have been against the rules, but it was good for me. My self-confidence grew because of her attention.

"We made each other laugh by teasing the other nurses and playing tricks on my mom. Nicole helped me realise that I could either feel sorry for myself and cry about my situation or I could laugh and make the most of my life. I chose to laugh.

"I hated the evenings. If something went wrong during the day, my mom and Nicole were there. At night I'd get nervous of the respirator stopping. I couldn't call for help because the trachey was in my throat.

15

Once or twice the machine stopped and I'd start losing consciousness, but the machine would beep and the nurses would rush in. I practised clicking my tongue to call for help. I got very good at making this sound: I could do it quite loudly.

"It was during those evenings that my helplessness, my utter dependence on other people, began to sink in. I was forced to be alone with my thoughts, no people popping in and out to distract me. During the day my friends visited often; we joked and laughed and talked about old times. It was easy to forget I was a quadriplegic; I didn't think about how much pain I was in.

"In the evening, though, when I was lying in bed, staring at the ceiling, there was no one to chat to. That's when my thoughts started to haunt me. Thoughts about the permanence of my situation; fears for the future. How were we going to cope at home? What would happen to me if my mom wasn't there to look after me any more?

"A lot of people have sleepless nights, worrying themselves enough to turn molehills-sized problems into mountains. At least when they wake in the morning they can regain perspective, turn those mountains back into molehills. But my problems really were the size of mountains, and I knew the next morning they wouldn't be any smaller. And at night, I couldn't get away from them. I couldn't pick up a book or turn on the TV, or get up to exercise, or even fetch a glass of water. It was just me and my thoughts; those nights would drag. It would have felt like an hour had gone by, but when I looked at the clock only a minute had passed. Time would hang.

"Then, just as I was starting to drift off, I'd be woken by a pipe being shoved down my throat to suction out the phlegm. I'd have to start the battle to fall asleep all over again. It would get stifling hot and dry and I'd get thirsty, but I couldn't reach out my arm for a glass of water.

"I was at the mercy of a nurse for everything. It all used to be so easy, but now every little thing had to be planned to the last detail. My life was not going to be the same. I had to make a switch; I had to come to terms with this new life, and make the most of it.

16

"Most school-leavers don't know what they're going to do with their lives, but I did. I knew what I wanted: I was going to be a South African cricket player. But all of a sudden there I was, 19 years old and, like everyone else, with no clue to what I could do with the rest of my life. But unlike other 19-year-olds, however uncertain, I was also paralysed."

Then Victor received a letter from one of his coaches. "He reminded me of the time, in a match against Free State, I'd been hit in the eye by a cricket ball. Even though my eye was cut open and bleeding, I went to bat again. He told me to face this setback as fearlessly as I'd faced Free State's fast bowlers. After I read the letter I resolved to make the most of my life. Maybe one day medical research will come up with a cure, but I decided that there's no point in waiting for that day. I have to make the best of my life now, as a quadriplegic."

18

CHAPTER 3

Dancing into the World

"My parents named me Victor. They had no way of knowing how prophetic that name would be. I believe there is a victor that lives in each one of us. Sometimes, this victor emerges only when we are confronted by seemingly impossible challenges."

Vic was born on July 16 1973. He was named Victor Ben Ned Vermeulen and looked, Isabella says, like a marshmallow. His skin was white, his cheeks were pink, his eyes blue and his hair was red.

On the way home from the hospital Tokkie, Victor's father, stopped about 50 times to examine his baby boy. When they got to their home in Melville he took the baby and marched into the house, forgetting Isabella in the car.

Victor was danced into the world, Isabella remembers. "Tokkie and I loved to go dancing. We danced all the way through my pregnancy until just before I gave birth.

"Once, when Vic was about five months old, I was sitting with him on my lap, talking to Tokkie's mother. We were playing a record: *She's a Long Legged Woman Dressed in Black*. I noticed Vic was moving back and forth. I thought something was wrong with him. My mother-in-law raised seven children, and I was always consulting her on child-care. As a first-time mother, I was a little insecure. But this time she also didn't know what was wrong with Vic. She's never seen anything like it. Out of the seven she'd raised, not one had moved like that. Then the record stopped, and Vic stopped moving. I put it on again, and he started to move again. We realised that he had been swaying to the music. Dancing, at five months!

"He loves music; he really did have natural rhythm. While I was pregnant, Vic must have come to know and enjoy the flow of music from inside me."

Little Vic joined a family made up of Tokkie, Isabella and his 14 year-old half-brother Eddy, as well as Sheila, Tokkie's stepdaughter from a previous marriage, and her husband Big Vic. Sheila is a year older than Isabella; she and Big Vic lived in an upstairs flat in the Vermeulen household. The couple couldn't have children, so Tokkie decided to name his son after his stepdaughter's husband. Little Vic called his stepsister Mama Sheila. "Everyone used to expect this big "mama" to come out, but Sheila was as thin as a pin," recalls Isabella. The Vermeulens were a close, affectionate and very demonstrative family, always touching and hugging each other.

"Those seemed perfect days," says Victor. "On weekends I'd wake up, run into my parents' room and jump on their bed to wrestle with my dad. Once I dived onto the bed and I broke the base clean in half.

"I was extremely fortunate to have had parents like mine. They gave me their love, their support and their time. But the best presents my parents ever gave me were the values of self-confidence and the drive to win.

"This inner belief and my desire to succeed has helped me come to terms with my accident. Learning to accept my paralysis is one of my greatest achievements; not allowing myself to become a bitter victim of circumstance, bogged down by resentment and anger. My experience in life has taught me a lot about the tools we all need to unearth the winning qualities that lie within us; qualities that give us all the potential to become victors. I may be disabled, but I am still a winner - a victor.

"All of life's victories start with a vision. To be truly happy and fulfilled, you have to follow your own vision.

"My vision began in my backyard when I was about three years old. My older brother was playing cricket with his friends, and I remember thinking that I liked everything about this game - the smell of linseed oil on the bat, the feel of it in my hands, the sound it made hitting the ball, the crackling heat of the highveld afternoon - everything. Watching them play made me feel happy inside; more than anything else, I wanted to be big enough to play with them."

Victor had an exceptional sporting talent and cricket became the focus of his energy. He was a prodigy, even as a toddler, and from a very young age resolved that one day he would become a great cricket star. With pudgy little legs Victor chased dreams and cricket balls.

Red-brown spiky hair, hazel-green eyes, knees covered with grazes and bruises, Victor, extroverted and carefree, always wore a warm smile. He was an active, accident prone child whose early years were peppered with frequent visits to the hospital.

At eight months, Victor had been up all night, screaming. In the morning, he was taken to the doctor who told Isabella that her son needed an operation to remove abscesses that had developed in both his ears. If the abscesses had burst he would have been deaf.

At 19 months, Victor fell off a chair in the hair salon where Isabella worked, banged his nose on the wall and broke it. A month later, Isabella wasn't feeling well and went with her son to see the doctor. The doctor saw Victor and told Isabella to rush him to the Garden City Clinic at once. Victor had an abnormally long appendix that had to be removed. That night Isabella slept on the floor of the hospital next to Victor's cot.

When Victor was three and a half Isabella glanced through a window and saw her son outside, standing on top of the gate and then jumping. He got up, brushed the dust from his clothes and ran off happily. She thought nothing of it. He was playing with his cousins. What she didn't know was that their game was to see who could jump from the highest point.

"I always had to be the best," says Vic. "I couldn't give in. I hated losing. My cousins were older and much bigger than me, but I was going higher and higher and jumping." Victor, three years old, ended up jumping off the roof.

"He was always in trouble, this kid," remembers Isabella.

"I had no fear of anything," says Victor.

"He had a will of his own."

That night he was fine, but the following morning when he tried to get out of bed, his legs crumbled beneath him. Once again, Isabella had to rush him to the doctor. An X-ray revealed that Victor had pulled his leg right out of the socket. Doctor's orders were to keep Victor in bed for four months. This wasn't so easy with an unstoppable three-year-old like Vic.

"I remember lying in bed, all my friends and cousins playing outside. My mom gave me puzzles and read to me and we listened to records, but it wasn't the same. It was very frustrating." Vic pauses, and gives a quick grin. "I think now, maybe the big guy upstairs was preparing me. Maybe he wanted to see if I could handle the situation."

When Victor recovered, the family went to visit Isabella's brother on his Standerton farm. There were miniature Doberman puppies on the farm, and Victor fell in love with one of them. Isabella said Victor could have it if he promised to take care of it.

"I explained that this meant cleaning the puppy's poops. 'It is your responsibility now,' I said. Victor promised he'd look after the dog, which he named Mickey.

"When we arrived home I noticed that every five minutes Vic would run into the bathroom and then run out again. In and out. It went on the whole morning. Finally I spied on him to see what mischief he was getting up to. Every time the dog pooped, Vic was there with toilet paper, actually wiping the dog's bum."

Vic remembers another bathroom adventure. "One evening, when I was five, Big Vic poured my dad a heavy brandy and Coke. My dad wasn't a big drinker; it was a bit strong for him so he left the drink. I'd been playing outside and when I came in I saw the Coke and took a sip. 'Ooh, this is nice,' I thought, and gulped down the rest.

"About fifteen minutes later, my dad called me. I came to the room, walking strangely and slurring my words. My mother took me to the bathroom because my stomach was upset. I was sitting on the toilet, saying to my mom, 'Oh. Mom, I love you.' I was suffering from a severe hangover. My mom laughed and the more she laughed the more upset I became."

Isabella laughs now, remembering. "Here's this little thing, balancing himself on the toilet. I'm sitting on the side of the bath, hanging onto him so that he doesn't fall off the toilet and holding a pot because he's puking and his stomach is running at the same time. And he's telling me how much he loves me!"

"The more I told my mom how much I loved her, the more she laughed at me," says Vic. "I got very upset. I didn't think it was funny.

"Then my brother Eddy came into the bathroom to see what was going on. He was really worried about me, throwing up, my stomach running, acting strange. So I started on him.

"'Eddy, Eddy, I love you,' I wailed. My dad was laughing at me, my mom was laughing at me, but Eddy didn't laugh. So I told him: "Eddy, you're the only one who loves me!"

Victor was raised by parents who doted on him but did not spoil him, who encouraged him but did not make him feel entitled, who taught him the importance of expressing his individuality while at the same time understanding the value of team spirit. It was his parents' love, his charisma and his natural physical talent that carried him through a carefree childhood.

"When Vic was four I took him to see *Saturday Night Fever*. When we came out, Vic said to me, 'Mommy, if you buy me that record I'll dance like John Travolta.' His half-brother Eddy had a copy, so we put the record on and Vic started to dance. I couldn't believe it. The child had such rhythm. He did Travolta's whole *Staying Alive* sequence beautifully, wiggling his little bum and pointing his fingers at the heavens. He absolutely loved performing, he revelled in being in the limelight.

"One day I took him to a big department store and he promptly got lost. I ran around the shop looking for him until I noticed a crowd of people had gathered at the record bar. I knew immediately that Vic

23

was somehow involved. I pushed my way through the crowd and there he was - swaggering, boogying, bopping and leaping into the air. The crowd was intoxicated. Here was a boy clearly born to perform. He launched into his *Staying Alive* routine and the crowd laughed and clapped. He was such a crowd-puller the floor manager asked me to bring him back, offering to pay Vic to dance at the shop at the weekends."

"I was lucky," says Victor. "I'd see something once and be able to do it. Like riding a bicycle. My parents gave me a bicycle when I was three and I insisted they remove the training wheels. My dad took me to some sports fields to teach me how to ride. I jumped on the bike, grabbed onto a rugby pole and told my father to push me. He refused. 'You're going to fall,' he warned. I begged in a way only a child can beg. Finally my dad pushed, and I rode off on the bike without a wobble. He was flabbergasted. He ran home to fetch my mom to come and look.

"It was the same with anything. I was fortunate; I had very good co-ordination. When I was 12 my father bought me a four-iron golf club. I had never played golf before. We went for a game at the golf course and I broke 100. People can play hundreds of games of golf and never break 100. Sport came naturally to me. I was fearless and strong-willed."

Vic's determination often translated into sheer stubbornness, which showed itself very early. Vic's stepsister Sheila recalls how bloody-minded her kid brother could be.

"Vickie always knew what he wanted, from a young age. When he was four I took him with me to the Oriental Plaza. After some shopping we went to a restaurant to get something to eat. I ordered him a hamburger and a milkshake. He refused to eat it. 'No,' he said. 'I want curry and beer.' He was determined. It was curry and beer, or nothing. He had made up his mind and there was no changing it.

"I also remember that Vickie would always be waiting by the gate, a bat in his hand, for Eddy to come home from school. 'Come boet, come boet, bowl to me.' Eddy would bowl to him for hours. We all used to play carpet bowls. Vic was always very competitive. His motto was: If I do it, I want to win."

But Victor was also a caring boy. One afternoon, screaming down Melville Hill on the yellow skateboard his parents bought for his third birthday a few months earlier, Vic saw a woman who looked very sad and miserable.

He stopped and said hello, asking if he could help. She told him she was looking for a job. Victor told her not to worry: he'd find her a job. He marched up the hill, skateboard under his arm and the woman a few steps behind, knocked on his mother's door and told her to employ this nice woman. "No, Vic," said Isabella. "I'm not hiring." But Vic was insistent. "Come on, she's nice!" Isabella finally relented and agreed to give the woman a one week trial. Twenty-five years later Maggie Keebine still works for the Vermeulens, and is very much part of the family.

All Victor's friends were older than him. When they went to school, Victor had no one to play with, so he too wanted to go to school. He begged and pleaded with his mother until she put his name down on the waiting list of a nursery school near their house. Three months later, when Victor had made new friends and was no longer desperate to go to school, the nursery school phoned to say that they had a place.

"On my first day we stayed indoors singing, cutting out shapes and colouring in. After lunch, just when I thought the teacher was going to lead us all out into the playground, she made us lie down for a nap! A nap, in the middle of the day! I was disgusted. I didn't come to school to sleep. I wanted to play cricket, I wanted to play Superman, I wanted to play all day. Napping only got in the way of the fun.

"I came home that first day and said to my mom, 'I've got news for you, I'm not going back to that school.' My mom said, 'I've got news for you, I've paid the deposit and you are going back to that school.'

"So on the second day, during nap time, I snuck out of the classroom while the teacher was distracted. I crawled under a little fence, scaled a two metre wall and sprinted home. I started my bunking days early.

"When I got home I hid under my mom's brass bed and I said to Maggie, 'Please don't tell mommy that I'm here.' Maggie went straight to my mom and said: 'Ma'am, die Vic is hier.' Then my father came home early and I crawled out of my hiding place and said: 'Dad, you can hit me, you can kill me, but I'm not going back to that school. I've made up my mind. They make me sleep when I don't want to sleep.' My dad thought about it, and then said I didn't have to go back to school.

"Then my dad noticed a woman outside our house. It was my teacher, looking for me. He invited her in, and told her that he was allowing me to stay home from school. But she was having none of it, and insisted on speaking to me. My parents took her to me and as soon as she walked through the door I started to scream at her.

"'Get out!' I yelled. 'Get out of my house!' I really didn't want to go back to that school. All the adults were really taken aback."

Vic was amazed his father had let him off so easily. Tokkie Vermeulen always emphasised to his son the importance of finishing something once he had started it. But he did give Vic a warning.

"Next year, you are going to school whether you like it or not. You're going, even if I have to kick your bum all the way there."

"I was enrolled at Melville Primary School, and I was excited, because I really liked the school. Then my father was transferred to Pretoria. I wasn't too keen on this, because I was leaving Mama Sheila, Big Vic and all my friends. I also had to go to North Ridge Primary, in Pretoria.

"I wasn't keen on North Ridge, because I'd been so excited about the Melville school. But my mother was crafty. The first time we visited the school it was the prize-giving day, with cakes and tea for the parents and children. My mother said, 'Look, Vic, what a nice school this is! They give you tea and cakes every day!' I soon discovered otherwise, but I didn't care because I was having such a great time. I really liked North Ridge. I ran that school."

"From his second day of school Victor decided that he wanted to catch the bus to school and back home again," remembers Isabella. "I made sure he got on the right bus and then I drove behind it to make sure he got off at the right stop. That afternoon he confronted me: 'I saw you following the bus. You don't have to follow the bus! I'm not a sissy. I can go to school on my own!'"

"I couldn't bear to let anyone think I was a sissy," says Vic. "Before I went to school, my mom took me for swimming lessons. I didn't want to learn to swim. I suppose it might have been a good thing if I hadn't learned. I've had two pool accidents: I cracked my lower vertebra during a water polo game in high school, and then, of course, when I was 19 I dived into a swimming pool and broke my neck.

"My mom took me to swimming lessons but I wasn't too keen. The next swimming lesson I told my mom that I didn't really want to go, that I was only learning to swim because the family wanted me to. But when we arrived at the pool my mom said if I didn't get in the pool people would think I was a sissy. That changed my mind. Nobody could think I was a sissy. I jumped into the pool faster than you can say breaststroke and I learned how to swim."

Vic's determination and ability to succeed at whatever he tried paid off in other ways. At one point his mother was making a table out of marbles. In order to help her, Vic would go to school every day with an extra, empty lunch box. Each break he'd play marbles with the other boys, invariably relieving them of their marbles every time. And so he'd go home at the end of the day with that extra lunch box filled with marbles, for his mom.

In the family's first year in Pretoria Victor got another miniature Doberman. Mickey, the dog whose bum Vic wiped, had died and they got another dog, which Vic also named Mickey. Mickey was to discover that being around Vic was also not for sissies, Isabella remembers.

"Vic was playing in the back yard when he suddenly came running into the house, screaming. I ran outside to see what was going on, and saw little Mickey lying on the grass. I picked him up: he wasn't moving. Vic thought he'd killed his dog; he ran off, screaming.

"He'd been playing cricket and when his friend bowled the ball, the dog chased it. The ball and the dog arrived at the same time Victor smashed a cover drive. He smacked the dog on the nose with the bat and knocked the poor thing unconscious.

"I found Vic sobbing his heart out under a bush. We rushed Mickey to the vet, who said that the dog should be put to sleep. He said Mickey didn't have a chance. I explained that if the dog died Victor would think he had killed it, and that would destroy him. The vet shrugged. He gave me a dropper and some medicine and told me I had to dose the dog every two minutes. I stayed up all night with that dog. I never slept. The next day I took the dog with me to work and I cuddled it and dosed it with the dropper. I did this for a few days and the dog recovered. After that, poor Mickey's head shook slightly, but otherwise he was fine."

Vic smiles all the way through this story. When his mother finishes, he says, "See, she stayed up all night for that dog. That was God's way of testing her, to see if she could get up at night to look after me."

When Victor was eleven, the school phoned to tell Isabella she had better come quickly because her son had been in an accident and needed to go to hospital.

"I got to the school and found Vic in the sick bay - he had a hole in his head so big I could have put my whole thumb into it. He'd been teasing a girl and she had chased him with a compass. Running away, he fell over a suitcase and hit his head on the brick wall.

"After going to the doctor to be stitched up he wanted to go back to school. He never missed a single day of primary school. His High School, though: that was another story."

Primary School saw the start of Vic's glory days as a cricketer. And it all started with a very special cricket bat: a Duncan Fearnley Magnum. Vic remembers that bat fondly.

"I was in standard two, my mom and I were browsing in a sports

28

store, when I saw the Duncan Fearnley Magnum. My heart raced. I picked up the bat and held it in my hands. I wanted it.

"My mom saw the look in my eyes and shook her head. There had been a change of ownership at the food distribution company where my dad was the manager and my dad had been retrenched.

"'Mom,' I begged, 'please buy me this bat. If you buy it for me I'll score so many hundreds.' My mom shook her head again and told me gently that we couldn't afford it. 'Let's go,' she said.

"I asked if I could just look at the bat for another five minutes. Five minutes later my mom wanted to go, but again I pleaded for another five minutes. It was such a beautiful bat: I couldn't bear to leave it. Eventually my mom managed to get me away from the bat and out of the shop.

"Before Christmas my mom put my present under our Christmas tree and my friends and I tried to guess what it was. We couldn't. I remember when Christmas finally arrived and I opened the box. I pulled out a jersey and then, wrapped in another jersey, was the superb Duncan Fearnley Magnum bat. I let out a yelp, I kissed my mom and then I buried my head in my father's neck and burst into tears. I howled. My mother started crying. My father started crying. The three of us sat there, sobbing.

"Out of all the bats I have ever played with that was my favourite. The next year, when I was in Standard 3, I scored my first century with that bat."

There was a North Ridge tradition that if any boy scored a century, the school would buy him a new cricket bat. Until Victor Vermeulen arrived it had been a pretty inexpensive tradition: no boy had ever scored a century in the 11 years of the school's existence. It's very difficult to get high cricket scores at the Standard 3 level because only 25 overs are played per side. But Victor did it - once in Standard 3, four times in Standard 4 and four times in Standard 5. After the third time the headmaster said to him, "You don't need any more bats! Anyway, we can't afford it - you're bankrupting the school!"

Vic's headmaster recognised the talent in the young pupil. From

Standard 4, he took Victor into the hall and threw tennis balls at him so Victor could practice his cricket strokes.

"The headmaster loved me. I was once sent with two other pupils to the headmaster's office to be caned. The headmaster caned the other two boys then called me into the office, closed the door, told me to bend over and he hit the chair. He said go tell them that you've been jacked. Up until now those guys still think I got jacked that day with them."

Three years in a row Vic won the Sportsman of the Year Award, as well as awards for Most Dedicated Sportsman and the Victor Ludorum. Four years ago, North Ridge Primary instituted the Victor Vermeulen Plaque, a sporting award for courage and fighting spirit.

Victor was chosen to represent the Northern Transvaal province in cricket and soccer. He captained both the soccer and the cricket Northern Transvaal sides in Standard Five. Watching their son play sport was very important and Victor's parents never missed a match.

"My dad was a very friendly, warm-hearted person, and he and my mum would always wait until the last boy had been picked up from a match or practice. If a boy wasn't picked up, they would take him home. One day after practising with the Northern Transvaal soccer side, when I was about 12 or 13, there was a boy sitting on one of the benches and my dad and I were talking to him - my dad was 'one of the boys'.

"My dad saw he was sad, and asked him why. He turned around and said to my dad that his mum and dad had been divorced for some time; his dad had promised to pick him up after practice to go and buy him some football boots. His dad hadn't arrived. After waiting for his father for about an hour, my dad told the boy to gather his things. We got into the car and my dad stopped off at a sports shop, took him into the shop and bought him the best pair of football boots - the ones he'd had his heart set on." It was witnessing his father's acts of kindness that taught Victor integrity and compassion.

Victor was head boy of North Ridge Primary. Because of his sporting achievements, he was offered scholarships to half a dozen high schools all over the country. He chose St Stithians because he wanted to be in Johannesburg so that he could remain close to his parents and they could continue to watch him play sports.

Victor wasn't only skilled in sports, he was also in the choir and an accomplished public speaker. In his last concert at primary school he received a Gold Plus Plus award for the recitation of one of his poems. A note from the adjudicator read: "See you on the stage one day."

"I never had any intention of going onto the stage. I was determined to be a cricket player. But life does strange things. Now I am on the stage: my motivational talks are a stage performance, although I'm not acting. I'm sure the adjudicator never thought I'd be on the stage in a wheelchair."

CHAPTER *4*

One Breath at a Time

Four months after Victor was rushed to Johannesburg General Hospital and admitted into the intensive care unit, he was discharged and flown by helicopter to Pretoria's HF Verwoerd hospital to begin rehabilitation.

He couldn't be transported by ambulance because his neck wasn't completely stable and doctors feared that with the vehicle's constant bumping, Victor probably wouldn't be alive when it arrived in Pretoria. A little jolt could have done a lot of damage. Victor was tied to a stretcher and strapped into the helicopter. The roof of the helicopter was about 20 centimetres away from his head. He couldn't see out of the window which made him feel disoriented and the medication made him feel woozy. It was hot and windy and he felt terrible. When the helicopter landed he turned his head and vomited.

Victor had left behind two safety nets: Nicole, the nurse who had been so caring, competent and affectionate to him, and that little mark on the ceiling which had given him a sense of security. He knew, however, that it was time to move on. His life was no longer in danger, thanks to the medical treatment he had received at the Johannesburg hospital. Now he had to learn how to adjust to his new set of circumstances.

"I felt as if my mind was being held prisoner in an immobile shell and I'd become frozen inside my skin. I couldn't do much, but I had made my choice. I wasn't going to just give up and die. I decided that my life was worth living and I was going to make the most of it; one breath at a time and one day at a time. I've never been a person who gives up. I decided to fight.

"I was breathing by myself and now I had to learn to sit up again. I'd been flat on my back for four months. To prepare me for my first sitting attempt, the nurse put white stockings on my feet and strapped a belt to my stomach. This belt is similar to the ones fighter pilots wear at high altitude; it stops the blood from pooling down to the feet. This was a real danger for me: my blood circulation was very out of practice.

"I sat up and, despite the measures taken, the blood drained from my head very quickly and in just 30 seconds I became so dizzy and tired that I nearly passed out. It felt like I had just completed a Comrades Marathon. I slept the rest of the day. My neck was also in a lot of pain because this was the first time I held it up without any support."

"I shared a ward with three other quadriplegics: Anton, Wayne and Paulus. We chatted to each other about our problems and swapped quadriplegic stories; catheterising and bowel movements and spasms. It made me understand that I wasn't the only one in the world going through this nightmare. It also made me realise how easy it is to become disabled."

"Anton was a contractor who tiled roofs. He fell off a roof and landed on his neck. He could move his arms but his hands weren't very strong. He could get on and off the bed by himself and push himself down to physiotherapy. Just that gave him so much independence. In the evenings, if I needed to call a nurse, I'd wake Anton and he'd push the buzzer for me.

"Anton and I laughed a lot. We were quite good mates. He always talked about how he felt like a beer and was going to get someone to smuggle a beer into the hospital for him. One afternoon my family came to the hospital to have a braai and my uncle had brought a beer. I said to Anton, here's a beer, you're such a man, why don't you pound it?

"He drank the whole beer and promptly puked.

"The camaraderie we had reminded me of my cricket days, all of the guys together, getting up to no good, ragging each other. I think I missed that the most. With the guys at the hospital, I started to realise that in a way, I could still have that. I could still have friendship, companionship, good times.

"Another guy in the ward was Paulus. He was riding a bicycle and someone drove into him and that's how he became a quadriplegic.

"Wayne was hitchhiking with his brother and got picked up by some right-wingers on their way back from a meeting. Wayne and his brother got involved in an argument with the driver. The driver shot them. Wayne's brother died and Wayne was left paralysed with only movement in one arm."

"There was another guy in a ward near us who really struggled with the idea of being paralysed. Every night he would sob about the loss of his legs. He couldn't handle it. We tried to cheer him up and tell him that things would work themselves out, but he just bawled and bawled.

"The guy hadn't actually severed the nerves in his spinal cord - they were just bruised and swollen. Three months later, when the swelling went down, he got back everything, all movement, all sensation. He did what everybody who's ever been told that he'll be confined to a wheelchair for the rest of his life only dreams about. He walked out of the hospital."

"I remember he came to say goodbye and told us that the reason he was walking was because he had been so positive. After he left the four of us in the ward burst out laughing. Obviously being paralysed is not a walk in the park - if you'll pardon the expression - but when he was in our situation he was a big baby and we consoled him.

"It was just the luck of the draw that when he broke his spinal column his spinal cord was just bruised, not severed. It doesn't matter how positive you are, if you've severed your spinal cord you're still going to be paralysed."

Another result of spinal cord injury is that the damaged spinal cord does sometimes continue to carry motor messages to the body - very garbled ones. These result in spasms - uncontrolled shakes in the body that can sometimes be so bad they resemble convulsions. The spasms usually happen when the body is moved, but they can also be completely spontaneous. Vic has had spasms so bad that he was once thrown right off his bed. He landed on his stomach and, face down on the floor, nearly suffocated. Since then his mother straps him into his bed every night.

"One religious man swore I would walk again if I chose a meaningful day on which I would walk, recite specific bible quotes every day and believe. I set a date, I recited the quotes religiously and I believed, but on the day that I was supposed to walk, I didn't. The man was unimpressed. He told me that the reason I hadn't walked was because my faith wasn't strong enough. He never came back."

It's very fortunate for Victor that he is self-confident and that he has a strong support system, because raising hopes for them only to be dashed can prove exceptionally damaging. It's not difficult to understand why a person who has been recently paralysed is so vulnerable and desperate and will seek hope wherever he can.

"One of the hardest things to deal with was friends who felt awkward about my situation. My macho cricket-playing friends would go white like a sheet and my 5'2" mom would have to comfort them. They used to become nauseous and leave the room very quickly.

"I don't blame them. I understand that they just couldn't bear to see me in such pain and so disabled. I explained that I'm exactly the same person that I was before the accident; I just can't move. I also tried to make them feel more comfortable by telling jokes about my circumstances and teasing myself. This put them at ease, because they could see that I was coming to terms with my predicament and if I could come to terms with it, then so could they.

"It hurt, though, when friends were reluctant to talk about the things they'd been up to; parties, sports, girls and big nights out with the boys, because they thought that I'd be resentful. Maybe I was a little resentful, but it was also important for me not to be shielded from the outside world."

Victor's first excursion back into the outside world occurred when nurses, occupational therapists and physiotherapists from the hospital took about twenty quadriplegics and paraplegics to a Pretoria mall to see a movie.

"The point of the exercise was a trial run to see what it was like being a cripple. I say the word 'cripple' but I'm not a cripple because I feel like a normal person although I can't move, but that day I felt like I was crippled.

"The purpose was to boost our confidence, but it actually served to give me an indication of how tough my new life was going to be, how vulnerable I was. It was my first time out in public as a quadriplegic and I could feel people staring at me. It was also my first introduction to the struggle of being in a wheelchair. There were no ramps and we had to be tipped onto and off the pavement. People didn't look where they walked and somebody bumped into me. At that point I didn't have a sense of balance and a little knock could have sent me sprawling. Of course, I can't put out my hands to break my fall either."

"The movie we all wanted to see was showing in a theatre at the top of a flight of stairs. We couldn't all get up, because there was just one tiny lift that could only take one person in a wheelchair at a time. But there were about 20 of us in wheelchairs. If we all took the lift, by the time the last person got up, the movie would be nearly over.

"Only seven people made it to that movie and the rest of us had to make do with the movie showing downstairs. We had to sit in the aisle of the movie theatre because no chairs had been removed to make room for our wheelchairs. There were also three steps that we had to be lifted up. When the movie was over we had to wait for the seven people to come down again. Unfortunately, the lift that had taken them up was no longer working. The centre's management had

37

to call a technician to fix it. The whole episode was a tremendous task."

"Later that evening I was listening to my beat box and Bette Midler's song The Wind Beneath My Wings began playing. It's a song about heroes; for me the song was about my mom. I listened to the words of the song and I knew that with thanks to my mom, and thanks to Maggie, who's like a second mom, I would be okay.

"I'm very fortunate to have a mom like mine; a no-nonsense red-headed woman with a fiery spirit and tons of love. When I was a baby, my mom fed me, bathed me, carried me, sang to me and made me laugh. Once again she would have to look after me because I'd become as dependent as a newborn baby. The only difference is that now I'm 6'3".

"As I drifted off to sleep, the words of the song turning over in my mind, I realised that having somebody to support me is a very special thing. A lot of people don't have that; and those that do, take it for granted.

"I don't take Maggie and my mom for granted. I know I'm really lucky."

CHAPTER 5

Cool Runnings

It is December 1985. PW Botha is South Africa's State President, Nelson Mandela is in prison, the country is under the grip of a State of Emergency while the black townships erupt in rebellion. The future is uncertain. Elsewhere, the Berlin Wall still divides Germany, there are no McDonalds stores in Moscow, and you'll need an e-stamp to send an e-mail.

Twelve-year-old Vic Vermeulen is standing in front of the mirror, dressed in his cricket whites. Recently graduated from North Ridge Primary, Vic is playing in the annual inter-provincial under-13 Perm Week. It's the morning before he is to play his last match for Northern Transvaal.

He feints with his bat, checking out his moves in the mirror.

"No fear," he tells himself. "No fear."

Victor Vermeulen doesn't fear a thing. After all: Life's a lag. The world outside may be in turmoil, but 12-year-old Vic knows what he wants. He wants good times, happy times. As he shadow-bats at the mirror, Vic thinks of his mates, thinks of the laughs they have together, thinks of ways he can make them laugh. Then his eyes narrow slightly. His small frame seems to straighten, and each swing he makes at the mirror, at a ball only he can see, becomes more precise. More than anything, Victor wants to win.

He takes guard. Poised. Eager. Thrilled. One ball left in the innings. Six runs needed for Northerns to win. Vermeulen to bat. The bowler steams in. It's a fast and short ball. Attack. Vic swings the bat and the ball sails over the boundary. It's a six.

"Yes," he tells himself. "Yes. Brilliant."

Vic Vermeulen is twelve years old, and he knows he can play cricket. More than that, he knows he has the talent and the drive to play for his country, for South Africa, and win.

Vic was captain of the Northern Transvaal team, and that last match, played against Free State, was won by Northerns. A Sunday newspaper report captured the talent of a young Victor Vermeulen:

It's a pity that Victor Vermeulen will be lost to Northern Transvaal high schools cricket over the next five years. He showed up a weak Free State bowling attack to score a solid 63 in Northern Transvaal's total of 153. Vermeulen, captaining Northerns, attacked the bowling at every opportunity.

Also playing at that Perm Week festival were Nicky Boje, Adam Bacher, Dale Benkenstein, Herschelle Gibbs and Shaun Pollock. Ten years later these men would have all been selected to represent South Africa.

Andrew Kramer, a left arm spin-bowler for the under-13 Transvaal team, recalls the Perm Week festival. Vic Vermeulen was a lanky, good-looking fellow who already had a reputation as a fearless batsman. When Mark Weinstein bowled a ball that creepy-crawled innocently along the ground until it slammed into Vermeulen's stumps, the Transvaal team was overjoyed.

"We were happy we got the danger man out so cheaply. It was a lucky wicket. We were 12, 13 years old, and all highly competitive.

"At lunch each province would huddle together and ignore the other teams. Except for Vic. Unconcerned about 'lunching with the enemy', he came and sat at our table. It was such a non-conformist thing to do. He clearly just wanted to make mates. He sat down and started teasing Weinstein about the fluky wicket he had taken. 'You'll never do that again,' he joked.

"I was struck by Vic's confidence. We became good friends."

Vic took up the sporting scholarship offered by St Stithians College in Johannesburg. He stayed in the school's hostel because his parents were in Pretoria.

Vic loved the hostel: he was an extrovert, surrounded by friends all day. The only problem was the bells. Hostel life was run by bells: a bell to wake up, a bell for roll call, a bell for breakfast, a bell to brush your teeth. Vic, an independent spirit, hated having his life run by a bell. "It made me feel so boxed in," he recalls.

It was also compulsory for all hostel boarders to be in the choir. Vic had sung in his primary school choir, and enjoyed it. But High School choir was something different. Singing sweetly was not the most macho activity around, and like all 13-year-old boys, Vic took his manhood seriously.

So he deliberately croaked and crackled his way through the first choir practice. The teacher asked what was wrong with his voice. He told her it was breaking, and was excused from the choir.

Vic continued to establish himself as a schoolboy sports star, earning sporting awards and write-ups in local newspapers. Sport, in particularly cricket, had become his life.

"I loved school because of my friends and sport. I tolerated academic study," he explains.

While still in Standard Seven, Vic made the St Stithians first cricket team. This remarkable achievement was virtually unheard of at the school. He could do no wrong on the sports field. Off the field was another matter.

He was always in trouble with the teachers. If anything untoward happened, all fingers pointed at Vermeulen.

One of Vic's friends remembers a fight breaking out at the bottom of the Old Boys Club; a teacher accused Vic of causing all the trouble. The friend recalls the incident.

"I was very surprised when Vic was singled out for blame, because I happened to have been sitting with him having lunch in the dining hall when the fight broke out. Vic had absolutely nothing to do with it.

"He was a real sports genius; I believe the teachers thought he had a big head because of it. They wanted to cut him down to size.

"Vic was confident, but he was never arrogant. He was the most down to earth person you could hope to meet."

Vic was raised to value humility, inspired by one of his mom's sayings: Be the least and you'll become the most.

Some Matric and post-Matric boys also resented him: those who felt that this little whippersnapper had usurped their rightful places in the first cricket team. But Vic wasn't in that team by accident. His friend explains:

"He was one of the finest schoolboy batsmen in the country, a left-hander who batted with the gift of unchained youth. His innings were famous for being hard-hitting. We nicknamed him Turbo because he was so quick running between the wickets."

Vic was so good he was already getting sponsorships: cricket bat manufacturers Duncan Fearnley supplied his cricket equipment.

Andrew Kramer went to King Edward's High School (KES) and even though the two went to rival schools and competed fiercely on the field each year, they remained good friends. Andrew also got to know Vic's parents.

"His father was at every game Vic played, and we all loved him. I would like to think I was his favourite, but the truth is everyone was his boy. After the game he would come and say, 'Nicely bowled, Kramertjie'. It made me feel good. We looked forward to playing against Vic, because come tea time we knew we would have a good giggle with Mr. Vermeulen."

"His dad was the most incredible guy," agrees South African batsman Adam Bacher, also a KES boy. "He gave such great encouragement, not only to Vic but to all the boys. And the boot of Vic's mother's Ford Escort was always filled with tuck, which she handed out to everyone. She became known as The Pantry."

"The three of them were a beautiful family unit," Andrew continues. "Victor's parents didn't push him, they encouraged him. They knew he had the talent."

Vic was the King Midas of sport - all that he touched turned to centuries, tries and goals. In his first rugby match he scored seven tries against Sandringham High School.

The rugby had to be put on ice the following year when, during a water polo match, one of the Matric boys jumped off a diving board and landed with his knee in Vic's back. In tremendous pain, Vic clung to the side of the pool waiting for someone to help him out because he couldn't get out by himself.

He suffered back pain the rest of that year, but continued to play soccer, cricket and rugby - his teammates strapped his back before every game. He played because he didn't want to let his team down.

Vic didn't connect the water polo injury to his continued back pain. "I put it down to growing pains. I was in agony, but I gritted my teeth and carried on."

The next year, representing Southern Transvaal in a soccer match, Vic kicked the ball and his legs went lame. He crumbled to the ground and his dad carried him off the field.

Vic was taken to the doctor where x-rays revealed that the lower vertebra in his back had been cracked in three places. He had to stay off all sports for six months and was advised not to play contact sports. He went to physiotherapy to strengthen his stomach, back and shoulder muscles. Six months later, in the winter season, he started playing soccer and in the summer he resumed playing cricket and rugby.

In his third year at St Stithians, Vic's parents moved back to Johannesburg and Vic became a day scholar. He left St Stithians at the end of the year to finish his schooling at Jeppe Boys High.

"I met up with Victor at the St Stithians Rugby Festival," remembers Adam Bacher. "He had just left St Stithians and he was playing centre for the Jeppe's First XV rugby team. I was playing fullback for KES. Although Vic was no longer at the school, there were no bad feelings between him and the other St Stithians boys. He got on with everybody.

"There were about 200 boys sleeping in one hall. Late one evening, Vic woke us all up and said that he had seen a couple on the field having sex. It was below freezing that evening, but he convinced us to go and have a look. It was a long walk to the bottom of the field and we were absolutely freezing.

"When we eventually arrived - eagerly expecting to glimpse some illicit liaison - there were no naked bodies in sight. We grumbled and then turned to Vic. He laughed. 'April Fools,' he shouted. He was always doing things like that."

Vic really enjoyed playing rugby. At Jeppe in Standard Nine and Matric he was selected to play in the Craven Week finals.

Vic also became known as the Cool Runnings guy. When anyone asked him how he was doing his answer was always, "Cool Runnings". This was before the Jamaican Bobsled movie Cool Runnings starring John Candy was released. Cool Runnings was Vic's own original way of saying he was doing great, life was fun and he had no worries.

Whenever he scored a try, the spectators would chant: "Cool Runnings … Cool Runnings … Cool Runnings." In a match against King David Linksfield High School, he scored a try and while the whole school began the "Cool Runnings" chant, Vic did the Michael Jackson moonwalk under the rugby poles.

Not satisfied with being a cricket prodigy and the coolest runner in rugby, Vic also excelled at South African Schools Soccer. So much so that when he was 15 Jomo Sono, the South African soccer legend, approached Vic to play professionally for his Premier League team, Cosmos. But although Vic loved soccer and was good at it, he declined the offer. He knew cricket was his true calling.

He was fast gaining a reputation as a resolute cricketer. The first time Natie King saw Vic at a cricket match was when he and Natie's son Greg were playing for Wanderers.

"That whole season everybody was talking about the talented up-and-coming wunderkind, Vic Vermeulen. It was Vermeulen this, Vermeulen that. There was a lot of hype about the boy's potential.

There was talk that he might become one of the giants of the sport.

"Everybody came to the match to watch Vic. He and Greg were batting at the crease. Vic was looking really good, and then something unexpected happened. He hit the ball, the two batsmen set out for a run, and collided in the middle of the pitch. They both fell to the ground. The fielder had no doubt at which set of wickets he should throw the ball. Taking Victor's wicket was the only way you could hope to win a match.

"He played very positive cricket. He was all heart. When I saw him that day I knew that this boy would succeed at whatever he did. I was right."

Andrew Kramer recalls bowling to Vic being something of a nightmare. "He would take guard, tuck in his chin, keep his head down and guts it out. He never batted with a helmet.

"He was the most feared batsman in the league. He tried to hit the ball further than the boundary necessitated. He was flamboyant and fearless. The innings he played were always all or nothing. And mostly, he would get it all.

"Vic was so good. He was better than guys who later made it to the provincial and national teams. I've coached some Transvaal sides and I've seen some very talented youngsters come through, but I don't think any of them were in Vic's league.

"A lot of good players average scores in the 40s and 50s during the school season, with one or two centuries. Vic scored seven or eight centuries - and they were big centuries, 160 and 200s. He had the West Indies flair, but he also had discipline, and he timed the ball to perfection. That's something only the real greats can achieve. It's something a person can't just learn - no matter how much he practises."

Then Vic set his sights on the Nuffield Week, an annual cricket festival for provincial teams drawn from high school teams. Each school selects a team to compete in the provincial selections and then each province chooses a team to play at Nuffield Week.

At the end of the week, out of thousands and thousands of cricketers in the country, the selectors choose just 13 boys to represent the South African Schools' side. The pressure to make the side is intense.

"In 1988, when I was in Standard Seven, I was selected for the Transvaal B side. The following year, I expected to make the A side, but I had a terrible week at the provincial trials and I didn't mange to score so many runs. However, because I had made the side the year before, the selectors picked me for the Transvaal B side.

"I wasn't feeling too good about it. I discovered something about myself: I hated to lose. I was determined to prove myself to the selectors and my friends. I decided that I was going to make the South African Schools' team.

"During Nuffield Week, I managed to chalk up a few good scores, but nothing outstanding. A batsman has to make a hellova lot of runs to be noticed and to be considered for the Schools' side. There were about a dozen teams and each one had five of their province's best batsmen. I had batted well, but I knew I had not batted well enough to make the side."

There was just one game, against Border, left in the festival. Vic knew this was his last chance. He had to produce something special.

It was clear that Vic had agility, speed and strength. But a lot of cricketers have those talents, and still don't succeed. What made Vic unique was his attitude. In cricket, the right attitude is a gift that conjures scoring magic out of mere physical ability. Vic was hungry, he had the desire and the discipline to succeed, to become a champion. He was as audacious as he was fearless.

Intense pressure, rather than intimidating him into bad form, heightened Vic's winning attitude. So in the match against Boland, Vic was in sparkling form. In just over three hours he hit 22 fours and a huge six to score an unbeaten 175 runs. Victor's masterful knock enabled Transvaal B to declare at 283 for four. Border was given the daunting task of scoring at a run rate of five to the over from the outset in order to win. The weather, however, had the final say. With Border on 99 for three, it began to rain.

Vic's score was the highest ever recorded at Nuffield Week since the festival began 47 years earlier. He beat the previous best scores held by Dave Robinson (166) and Graeme Pollock (153) - who was in the stands watching Vic's masterful innings. This record remains unbeaten to this day.

Vic was one of the youngest players ever to be selected for the South African Schools team. At the end of the festival, a sports journalist wrote that, while Victor "Turbo" Vermeulen may not yet be household name, "here lies the future of Transvaal cricket."

Two years later, playing for the Transvaal A team against Eastern Province during Nuffield Week, Vic clubbed 18 fours and four sixes to score 146 - the first century of the festival. Vic was selected four years in a row to play in Nuffield Week, and for three years running was chosen to represent the South African Schools side.

"It always struck me how strong Vic was," says Adam Bacher, who played Nuffield Week with Vic. "I was always very disappointed when he went out, because he played such good cricket, enjoyable cricket. He was amazing to watch. Vic was always slotted into the number-four position in the batting line-up. Traditionally, number four is the position where the most talented batsman in the team plays. If you look at the South African team, that's where Darryl Cullinan bats."

When he was 14, Vic played in the Johannesburg Premier Cricket League. His opponents were often men in their twenties and thirties. During one match, as Vic came in to bat, the bowler Paul Smith turned to him and asked: "Does your mother know you're here?" The whole team burst out laughing.

But they picked the wrong man to try to intimidate. Vic's razor-sharp tongue sprang into action. "At least I know where my mother is," he snapped back. The team laughed even harder. Vic had endeared himself to them. He was one of the boys. It's clear that from an early age, Vic learned to wield humour like a weapon.

But Vic's life wasn't only cricket. He relished his friends and had a huge appetite for good, clean mischief. He lived at full pace and his life was built around guts, respect, winning and having fun; lots of it. He didn't want to miss a moment of life.

Adam remembers Vic as a party animal. "I was actually scared to go out with him at night because he had so much energy. I was worried that I couldn't keep up with him. If the rest of us in the team had a big night like Vic, we would feel guilty. But Vic would party and never feel pressure - that was because he was so talented. We would go to sleep early, but Vic would be up all night having a good time. The next day he would still produce the high score of the match.

"I remember one evening in Grahamstown during Nuffield Week, we'd had a few drinks, and somebody dared Vic to run through a restaurant in his underpants. Nobody dares Vic. I looked up and he was off. He ran past three of the selectors. It didn't bother him because he was having a good time. I think the selectors secretly appreciated his courage, on and off the field. Needless to say he made the South African Schools' side that year."

Andrew Kramer also has stories to tell. "We only really started getting up to mischief in Standard Nine," he recalls. "In December 1990 he joined a bunch of us in Cape Town for a holiday. One night we were walking in town and we saw a gorgeous Capetonian and her monster boyfriend sitting in a BMW. Victor walked up to her, motioned her to unwind her window and then said: 'Hey cooks, I like your looks, I've seen your photo in the picture books.' We dragged him away before the boyfriend could fight.

"He was always at the centre of attention. He has an awesome exuberance for life. There's something about him that just attracts people. Women are crazy about him."

One of the women attracted to Vic was a pretty girl he had met when he went to Durban to play in a cricket tournament. The two kept in contact and one July holiday she came to Johannesburg to visit Vic. Vic took her to the White Horse Inn - one of his favourite clubs.

"We disappeared outside to neck behind some huts where the staff of the nightclub lived," Vic remembers. "After we'd been busy for a

▲ Age 2 already with ambitions to make the Springbok team.

◀ Mom & Dad in dance mode.

▲ At the beach.

▲
Gotcha! Playing for SA Schools in Cape Town.

◀ *Sportsman of the Year, Northridge Primary.*

▲ *Carrying the ball on the rugby field.*

◀ *Making my debut for Transvaal B in 1991 - 46 not out.*

Vic becomes the first batsman to make 100 at Nuffield week in 1991. ▶

▲ *Vic in action!*

▲ *With Mom and Dad.*

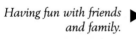
Having fun with friends and family. ▶

▲ *The team for the 1992 Transvaal Tour of England at Lord's Cricket Ground.*

▼ *My Transvaal team - Mom, me, uncle George, auntie Bernice, cousin Gisela.*

▲ *Autographs for the fans!*

A new life!

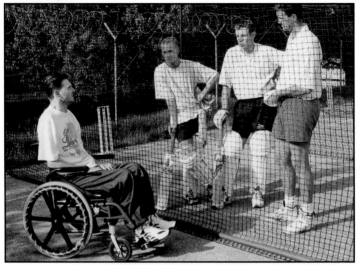

◀ *Coaching cricket.*

▶

On the MTN Roadshow - Maggie, Mom, Ann and me.

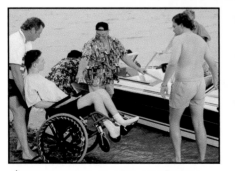

▲ *Unstoppable - trip in a speedboat - no problem!*

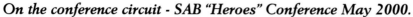

▲ *Nelson Mandela and
SAB Chairman, Norman Adami.*

▼ *My own particular hero.*

Painting by mouth.

▲ *Going home.*

▲ *The cricketer.*

▲ *A boat at Table Bay.*

▲ *Boks in the park.*

Photographs by Anne Brest.

while we decided to return to our friends. Then I discovered that someone had stolen my beige pants.

"I saw a pair of luminous green pants hanging on a nearby washing line. It was either this or going naked. I had no choice. I had to put them on. To make matters worse, they were so short they looked like knickerbockers on me. Wearing luminous green knickerbockers, I went back into the club to look for my friends. When they saw me they nearly killed themselves laughing. I didn't think it was so funny.

"But I couldn't go home in green pants. I'd have had to explain them to my mom. She always stayed up for me and she would have noticed if I'd arrived home wearing somebody else's trousers. I went back to the huts and discovered a pair of beige pants that looked similar to mine, and put them on. But they were also way too small; my mom would still notice.

"So when I got home, I pulled the pants I was wearing right down, pulled my jersey as low as possible and sprinted past my mom through the door, saying 'Ma, ma, I need to go to the toilet.' The next day Maggie covered up for me by getting rid of the pants. I saved up to buy another pair of pants so my mom wouldn't miss the beige ones."

"Most of my friends were people like me; people who grooved on life. We used to hang out at nightclubs, dance and chat and take pleasure in being young. We had no worries.

"There were always dance competitions at the White Horse. I would be watching the dancers when all of a sudden I would hear my name being called to dance. My friends knew I could dance well; they would enter me into the competition because they believed I would win. The prize was a bottle of Champagne and some money. My friends knew that if I won, a night of beers and burgers lay ahead of us."

Later, when Vic was selected to play for Transvaal, the cricket squad was invited to the opening night of the Health and Racquet Club at Old Ed's. The club hired professional dancers to perform. When the beat came on Vic couldn't help himself. "I jumped on stage with the dancers and boogied away with them. Eddie Barlow, the Transvaal coach, said to me, 'Vic, it's a pity your batting footwork isn't as good as your footwork when you're dancing!'" The dancers' trainer approached Vic, asking him to come and teach the professional dancers a few moves.

At 16 years old Vic, like most teenage boys, wanted nothing more than to be independent. He and a group of friends washed cars and did odd jobs so as to buy a second hand car, but it never panned out. Still, this longing for independence had its consequences, as Vic discovered one reckless evening.

"Chris, a friend of mine, had a crush on an American girl, and it was her last evening in South Africa. We were at Spats nightclub in Sandton; Chris asked me to drive him to visit her. I could drive a bit, but I was just 16 and unlicenced. I said no, but Chris nagged and nagged and eventually - against my better judgement - I gave in. He was a mate and desperately in love. I was just trying to help. We bumped into Stuart, a friend with whom I played cricket. He was 19 and owned a Golf. I asked if we could borrow his car, he nodded and handed me the keys.

"The drive to where the young woman's place was uneventful, but on the way back the roads were slippery because it had been raining. I took a corner too fast and slammed on brakes. The car started spinning. It hit the pavement, the tyres jammed and the car rolled three times - coming to a stop on its side in someone's garden."

"We crawled out of the car, shocked, but unharmed. A man came running out of the house, screaming, 'I've called the cops, I've called the cops.' I had no desire to spend a night in prison and adrenaline took over. I lifted the car by myself and pushed it upright. Chris stared at me as if I was the Incredible Hulk. 'Don't stare at me, help me push,' I shouted. The car's left wheel was ruined and the windscreen had come out. We put the windscreen on the back seat, jumped into the car and bolted.

"We drove down William Nicol Avenue and everyone was staring at us. We waved through the open windscreen. When we arrived

50

back at the nightclub, we parked the car, gave Stuart his keys and fled.

"It was wrong of us not to tell him his car had been wrecked, but we never really considered the consequences. We were 16-year-old boys.

"My nerves were frazzled and, to make matters worse, when we hitch-hiked home a maniac driver picked us up. I arrived home at about three in the morning, ready to sleep. A few moments later the doorbell rang. It was Stuart. He was furious. My mom and dad came to the door and I owned up. We went to Chris's house because my mom was worried that he might have been concussed.

"We had to face the music. We were grounded and we had to pay for the damage we'd caused. Looking back it was a wild and irresponsible thing to do. I could have so easily been paralysed; worse still is the thought that I could have been responsible for my friend being paralysed, maybe even dying. I would never have been able to live with myself if that had happened.

"We always feel our parents are being melodramatic when they try to protect us, but with the benefit of hindsight, I've learnt how important it is to think through the consequences of your actions; it could prove more than you bargained for."

CHAPTER 6

High Excitement and High Fives

Schoolboy one month, the next month Victor was tearing headfirst into a cricket career. As soon as he left high school he got a job as a chauffeur ferrying dignitaries and diplomats around Johannesburg. He was then snapped up to play for the Transvaal under-24 side. He accompanied the team on a tour of Natal. Vic's debut match was against an up-and-coming Natal under-24 team.

Adam Bacher, who had also been selected for the side, remembers the game well. "It was a very tense match. The 1992 Natal under-24 team was a phenomenal side, with Shaun Pollock, Mark Bruyns and Doug Watson in fine form. In that particular game another young cricketer, a powerful player from the surrounding farm area, was also making his debut. The man's name was Lance Klusener, also known as "Zulu".

"Victor was batting. He'd been there for a while and he was going beautifully. The game was petering out to a draw. Then his bat handle broke; he called for another bat. The boys in the change room brought him two bats: a regular bat and the one we called the Porno Bat."

Being a young side full of lads, some members of the Transvaal team had taped a picture of a naked woman from a Scope magazine centrefold to a bat. This was the Porno Bat.

Guess which bat Victor Vermeulen chose.

With a little nod and a glint in his eye, Vic grasped his bat and returned to the crease. The perky beauty on the bat pouted suggestively at the oncoming bowler.

"No one else would have had the guts to do it. We are all new kids in the team and we were trying to impress everyone with our serious cricket, but Victor had the courage. He wasn't scared of anything.

"The first ball he blocked and it hit the girl on her breasts. Vic said loud enough so the umpire and fielders could hear, 'Tit shot, hey?' The umpire nearly killed himself laughing. The next ball was a full toss - a loose ball that doesn't bounce and is easy to smack away to the boundary. Vic hit the ball right out of the grounds for a tremendous six. Again, he said loud enough for people to hear: 'Right in the sweet spot.' The bowler couldn't bowl because he was laughing so much and the umpire was forced to call for a drinks break."

The match was drawn, with Vic scoring 78 runs. It was a memorable knock.

Victor was then promoted to the senior squad and selected for the Transvaal B-side. Vic was progressing a lot quicker than the rest of the youngsters who had qualified through the schools system.

"Most of us were languishing in the junior sides," remembers Adam Bacher, "while Vic was making his presence felt. He was a remarkable person, a special person. He had a magnetic, sparkling personality: he just attracted people. And then he had this talent. Everybody was so impressed with his cricket. I hadn't reached that level yet. None of us had."

Vic played for the Transvaal B side in a five day match in the Free State against that province's B side. As usual, he played without a helmet. As part of Vic's No Fear trademark, he hadn't worn a helmet since he was a junior cricketer. Now that he was playing First Class cricket, that wasn't going to change. No fear, no helmet: it was the pride of youth.

It was the first innings and the bowler sent a bouncer down the crease. A bouncer is a ball which is pitched short and jumps up at the batsman. If a batsman spots it, he can either duck under it and let it go by harmlessly or position himself for a hook shot and send the ball sailing over the boundary for a four or a six. But if a batsman fails to spot the bouncer in time, the ball is likely to come blasting at his head. Bowlers hope that the batsman will raise his bat instinctively to defend himself and in the process nick the ball with the bat or get a top edge, and get caught out.

Vic hooked the bouncer for a one-bounce four. He was feeling cocky and had fallen into the bowler's trap. The bowler's next ball was another bouncer and Vic went to hook the ball for a six, but this delivery had been much faster and the ball rushed on to him. He got a top edge and the ball hit him straight on the top of his eye. "Worse still," says Vic, "I was caught."

"I walked off the field and into the change room. I looked in the mirror and saw blood and flesh pulsating out of a big gash above my left eye. I looked like a ghoul. My team-mates were nauseated, so I chased them around the change room, taunting them with my revolting wound. Then I was taken to the casualty for stitches. Let me tell you: a cricket ball is hard.

"That was my introduction to the First Class bouncer. I made it back in time for the second innings, but when I went out to bat I put on a helmet.

"For me, cricket is not just about the game. What stood out for me was the camaraderie in the change rooms and on the field. Guys on the field would chirp and sledge; it was like a performance. I miss the game, but most of all I miss the camaraderie. It was a time of high excitement and high fives."

Vic made his debut century when he was invited to play for Eastern Transvaal against the English county team Lancashire, and just four months after he had left school he was chosen to play in the legendary Transvaal A side against Worcestershire another English county team. Vic was one of the young lions to break through from the pack hungry for recognition at top level. He was chosen because when he played he gave everything, he battled and never gave up. He was at the top of his game. According to Anton Ferreira, a strong all-rounder who played for Warwickshire and Northern Transvaal, Vic's lack of inhibition attracted the attention of Transvaal coach

Eddie Barlow. "Barlow was always on the lookout for someone special. He was impressed with Victor's fire and passion," says Anton.

As a schoolboy, Vic had sat in the stands with his dad watching members of the Mean Machine (as the unbeatable team was once called) like Clive Rice, Jimmy Cook, Graeme Pollock, Henry Fotheringham, Ray Jennings, Alan Kourie, Vincent van der Bijl and Garth le Roux. Posters of them were taped to his bedroom wall and he'd queued for hours to get their autographs and shake their hands. Now Victor was also going to represent Transvaal. But there was a slight difference.

Those exceptionally talented cricketers had been lost to international cricket. Since the 1970s a sports boycott had been imposed by the rest of the world on South Africa because of the country's apartheid policies. Racist legislation that outlawed white and black from integrating politically, economically, religiously, academically and socially had caused South Africa to be expelled from world cricket. South Africa was in complete sporting isolation.

But this was 1992; African National Congress leader Nelson Mandela had been released from prison and the first shuffle to democracy was taking place. With the African National Congress and the National Party engaging in negotiating a political settlement, South Africa was just about to be readmitted into international sport. Vic was ready. He wasn't going to wait for the door to open for him, he was going to bash it down and march right in. Today Transvaal, Tomorrow ...

His selection to play against Worcestershire should have been the happiest moment of his cricketing career. Instead, the proud moment was marred by tragedy. Vic's father, Tokkie Vermeulen, was murdered.

CHAPTER 7

In Cold Blood

VERMEULEN
Henry (Tokkie) tragically killed. You will always be remembered for your kindness and zest for life and if we could have a wish today we would have you back in the same old way.

Tokkie, I loved the life we lived. Sweetheart, I loved the dreams we shared and all the things we did, but mostly I loved you. Your broken hearted wife Isabella and children Sheila, Eddy and Victor.

It's March 16 1992. Tokkie Vermeulen steers his bakkie down a dusty road in the dry rural town of Garankua. It's not yet 10 in the morning, and already the heat is unbearable. But Tokkie's mind is on his job. He has a particularly difficult client to deal with today.

Three days earlier, Tokkie turned 60. A sales representative for Springbok Wholesalers, a grocery supply company, Tokkie was the best rep in the game. He sold mainly to small family shops in the townships - black rural settlements, satellites of the wealthier and more established white towns. His job was to take the shopkeepers' orders for provisions, to be delivered later by Springbok Wholesalers. But to a lot of these small businesses, Tokkie was more than a sales rep. He didn't just supply groceries, he also helped shopkeepers manage their shops. He gave advice on the best deals, how to calculate supply and demand, and when to expect price hikes and discounts. The shopkeepers appreciated his advice. Tokkie was respected and well liked.

But the townships were becoming increasingly dangerous. A few years earlier he had been stabbed in an attempted mugging. On his birthday, Tokkie dropped into his stepdaughter Sheila's house for a cup of tea and told her that he was feeling very nervous. The situation in the townships was increasingly volatile. He felt he was in danger. Sheila suggested he find some other work. But that wasn't an option for Tokkie. "I'm 60 years old. At this age, what can I do?" he asked. In any case, he said, he was making plans to retire. He just had to stick it out a bit longer. After that, he'd spend his days following Vic's cricket career.

Tokkie was extremely proud of all his children: his stepdaughter Sheila and her husband Victor; his oldest son Eddy, his wife Anita and their two kids, Leanne and Neil; and Vic, his youngest son. The previous day he'd watched Vic notch up an impressive 50 runs for the Transvaal under-24 side against a visiting Australian Academy team. In just three days time Vic was due to make his debut for the senior Transvaal A side. He had been picked to play against the touring English county side Worcestershire. For Vic's old man it was a dream come true.

But he would never get to see his boy stride onto the pitch to play for Transvaal.

Tokkie negotiated the potholes in the dirt roads with practised ease. His musings were interrupted when he arrived at the shop owned by that difficult client. New to Tokkie's lists, the client hadn't paid for months. Tokkie's boss had insisted that this shopkeeper wasn't to be given any more supplies until he'd paid up. Tokkie had gone to see him and explained the situation. The shopkeeper agreed to pay and told Tokkie to come to the shop on Monday; the money would be waiting for him.

But on that particular Monday morning, it wasn't only the money waiting for Tokkie Vermeulen. At the shop, Tokkie noticed three men hanging about outside. There was something about their manner that he didn't trust. They seemed hyped; a little too eager. They were watching him a little too closely. He had enough experience to know that something wasn't right.

He decided that he would get the money and get out of there as quickly as possible. He walked into the shop, spoke to the client, collected the money and returned to the bakkie. As he was climbing into the seat, the three men pulled out firearms and started shooting. Tokkie was shot in the back. Somehow he managed to put the key in the ignition and start the bakkie. The men continued firing. As he drove off they shot into the bakkie, smashing the windows.

With four bullet wounds in his back and bleeding internally, Tokkie drove 15 kilometres to Garankua Bakery - a client of Tokkie's for the last 20 years. "Please help me," he said. "They shot me." His face was pale and he was leaning heavily on the bakkie door. He handed over the money he had collected and asked that it be kept safe and returned to his boss. Then he was rushed to Garankua hospital.

In the hospital, it was discovered that Tokkie's blood pressure was too high for the operation needed to save his life. He was medicated, and then left by himself on his hospital bed. He lay there, in the hospital, alone for three hours. He asked the nurse to phone his family. Then his boss Albert, and Bruno, a colleague, arrived at the hospital. Tokkie told them that he was alright, just in pain. Eventually his blood pressure was reduced sufficiently for him to be wheeled into the operating theatre. It was only when he was wheeled into the surgery that Isabella was eventually phoned. As Tokkie was pushed away he said to Albert and Bruno, 'Okay, I'll see you now-now.' Those were the last words he spoke.

In the operating theatre, Tokkie suffered a heart attack. The doctor stabilised him, but his blood pressure was still too high. He had another heart attack and died.

Eight years after his death, Vic talks about his father. Tokkie Vermeulen was an easy going, hard-working man, a wonderfully generous person. An enthusiastic sportsman, he played first division soccer until he was 42 and competed in the snooker league. But the real passion of his life was his wife and children. He loved his family.

"My dad was always next to the sports field watching me play," Vic recalls. "It didn't matter who we were playing and when; he was there. He would wake up early in the morning to finish his rounds in time for the match.

"We were a close family and the three of us always sat together on the couch. I remember we would fight each other to see who would be lucky enough to sit in the middle.

"The Friday before he died was my father's 60th birthday. My mom had decided not to have the usual big celebration with cousins, aunts and friends. Instead, on the Sunday, she gave an intimate supper, with just her and my dad, Sheila and Big Vic, Eddy and his family, and me. It was a wonderful, happy evening.

"That day, after I had scored 50 runs, my Dad congratulated me and told me how proud he was of me. He said he couldn't have received a nicer birthday present. Uncles, aunts and cousins were watching the match and as usual my mom (a.k.a. The Pantry) was feeding everyone. The game was drawing to an end when my mom said she was going home to make us a candlelight dinner.

"I had to drop my girlfriend, Ursula, and another friend at their homes, but instead I invited them for the supper and told them I'd drop them off afterwards. We had a lovely time. We chatted and we ate; my mom had made a scrumptious feast. I took my friend home and then stayed over with my girlfriend in Alberton.

"I'll always remember that when I left, my mom and dad were dancing up and down the kitchen. They were roaring with laughter. They looked so happy."

After Vic and his friends left, Isabella went to make some Milo. She asked Tokkie to put on a record. He chose Jim Reeves and when Isabella returned to the room she heard the strangely prophetic lyrics: *Now this is it / My time has come / Now this is it / The clock has stopped.* "It was as if he knew," says Isabella.

In the morning Vic returned with Ursula. "It was also strange, but I noticed that the big antique clock had stopped. My dad was always tinkering with that clock.

"Ursula and I were sunbathing on the front lawn. The phone had been ringing the whole day. It rang again and I don't know why, but I just knew something was wrong. My mom answered. I heard her saying: 'What? What?' There was a commotion. I ran inside. My mom turned to me. She was pale. 'Dad's been shot,' she said.

"We fetched Eddy in Pretoria and drove all the way to Garankua. As we walked into the hospital my mom went straight to the operating theatre where my dad was lying. She'd never been to the hospital before, but she knew exactly where to go. Through a window I could see my dad, lying on a hospital bed. His face was bloated. I burst into the room and called out to him, but he didn't reply. 'Dad, it's Vic,' I yelled. Nothing. I knew then that my dad was dead. A doctor came. He had blood on the front of his shirt.

"He directed us out of the operating theatre and into a side room. My mother, my brother and I. He started talking about time, like a schedule. It was bizarre. 'At 11h19 I did this and at 13h27 I did that.' It was unreal. I kept saying, 'Is my dad dead? He's dead, hey?' But the doctor never answered. He just kept giving times. My mom and Eddy were in shock. I don't think they realised what was going on. Eventually the doctor said: ' … and then at 15h21 we lost him.' I felt as if I had been winded. 'Son,' he said, 'your dad has been killed in cold blood.' I burst into tears. My mom and Eddy still looked dazed and confused. They didn't quite comprehend what was going on. We walked out of the little room into the passage where hospital orderlies had pushed my dad's body."

Isabella saw her husband. "He was lying there with his one arm curled behind him. He always slept that way. I wanted to talk to him. The doctor was telling me that they had done everything they could. I didn't know what he was talking about. It wasn't penetrating."

Vic takes up the story again. "They covered my dad's face with a sheet and pushed the trolley away. I walked next to it, holding on to my dad. They took him to the mortuary."

In the mortuary Vic stood at the bottom of the bed, rubbing his father's feet and saying: 'My dad, my dad, my dad.'

"Every evening, when my dad came home from work, his feet would be sore. Maggie would pour him a whisky, one whisky every evening to relax. Then he would lie on the carpet, put his feet on the couch and either my mom or I would rub his feet. He told me he liked the way I massaged his feet because my hands were strong. He'd put his feet in hot water and then I would push his toe until it cracked.

"In the mortuary, I pushed his toe and it cracked just like always. I walked out and left my mom alone with my dad for a few moments.'

Albert and Bruno came back to the hospital to see how Tokkie was doing. As they entered the ward they saw Vic crying. "Don't worry, man, dad will be fine," Albert said. "Dad's going to be alright."

"Dad's dead," Vic told them, but it didn't register. "No, no, your dad's going to be just fine,' Albert insisted. Eddy shook his head.

"We got home and the telephone rang. People had heard that my dad had been shot. They hadn't heard that he had died. When I broke the news to them they couldn't believe it. They had seen him the day before and now he was dead.

"You don't really realise that a person is gone for good until months, sometimes even years, later. We had a cat called Shammy who would always wait outside until my dad arrived home and then walk inside with him. My dad would lie down, waiting to have his feet massaged and Shammy would sit on his stomach and my dad would stroke him. For months, the cat lay outside, waiting for my dad to come home. Every night I would have to go outside to fetch the cat and bring him inside."

Vic and Isabella urged the police to investigate the possibility of a set-up. It was a significant coincidence that Tokkie had been killed just after receiving a large payment from a recalcitrant client. The police never came to take any statements and, despite Isabella nagging the police daily, the investigation did not proceed. Nobody was ever arrested and the murder docket was shelved.

Sheila, Vic's stepsister, remembers how Tokkie's death devastated Isabella and young Vic. "The three of them had been so close. I remember overhearing them one day a few weeks after Tokkie's death. Isabella had been crying inconsolably. Vickie came to comfort her. 'Mom,' he said, 'We loved dad and we miss him, but we've got to get on with our lives. You and I both know that's what he would have wanted.'"

CHAPTER 8

The Teen Machine

It was March 21 1992. As Vic woke up that Saturday morning, he felt a moment's intense excitement. Today was his first match in the Transvaal provincial team, his first step towards even bigger things. Once he had proved himself as a consistent scorer with big match temperament, it was just a hop, skip and jump to a place in the South African national squad.

Then he remembered, and his excitement vanished. All that remained was the sorrow. So much grief, it seemed to cover his body like a blanket of lead, smothering him. His dad.

He wanted to shout at the world. "It's not true," he wanted to yell. But it was true.

Today, of all days, his father should be, would have been, standing at the side of the field, watching him play. Witnessing his son's achievement, shouting encouragement, his grey head bobbing with excitement. But for the first time, Tokkie wouldn't be there. Vic would never see his father again.

There was a lot of media focus on the match because Damian D'Oliveira, son of former English cricketer Basil D'Oliveira, was in the Worcestershire side. Basil D'Oliveira, a brilliant batsman, was born in South Africa but as a coloured would have had no future in South African cricket in the apartheid era. So he went into exile in England, where he was soon selected to play for the English National squad. He was also to have an indirect hand in beginning the international sports boycott of his former country.

When D'Oliveira was selected to the English side that was to tour

South Africa in 1970, Prime Minister John Vorster was having none of it. He stood before the Orange Free State Congress of the National Party and announced to his delighted supporters that an English team that included a coloured South African would not be permitted to play in this country. The tour was abandoned, and Vorster's callous attitude sparked a disgusted outcry in the rest of the world, which led directly to South Africa's isolation from international sport for the next twenty years.

But now it was the 1990s and South Africa was on the road to democracy. The new generation of cricketers could look forward to full participation on the international arena. As Vic walked on to the field that day, it was an historic moment, for him and for his country. In this, his first match for the Transvaal, Vic was selected to open the batting. He took his place at the wicket, but he couldn't concentrate. He couldn't get his mind from the person who was missing from the stands, the person who really should have been there. It was Vic's most important match in his 12 years of competitive cricket - capped at every conceivable level and well on his way to playing for South Africa. And it was the first match his father would not see him play.

He got off to a cautious start, making only five runs before being run out. When the Worcestershire fielder picked up the ball for the run-out, Vic called on a little help from heaven. "Make him miss, dad,' he thought. Transvaal still managed to beat Worcestershire by 55 runs, thanks to a spirited 43 by Darryl Cullinan. Damian D'Oliveira took two wickets and scored eight runs.

Later that month Vic was picked for a tour of the United Kingdom with the Transvaal squad. This would be the very first tour to England taken by a South African provincial team since the end of the sports boycott. It was a young squad: the Mean Machine of the eighties had given away to the Teen Machine of the nineties. Under captain Jimmy Cook and coach Eddie Barlow, team philosophy was to accelerate the progress of young talent. It was a tour that demanded stamina; of the 18 days in Britain only four were not taken up by competitive cricket. Barlow imposed a rigorous training schedule. "We're not going for a holiday," he barked at his players before they left.

George, Tokkie's cousin, decided that he would take Isabella to England to watch her son play. When he phoned to let her know of his plan, Isabella demurred. "Thanks, George, but it's just too expensive," she protested. But Uncle George wouldn't take no for an answer. "Tokkie was so proud of Vic's achievements," he said. "He would have wanted to be there, but he can't. For Tokkie, you must go and watch Vic play."

Above Vic's bed in his Randpark Ridge home there is a framed photograph of the prestigious Lord's Cricket Grounds. If there is a place that is the centre of all the cricket played in the world, it is Lord's - the home of cricket. Lord's is owned by the Marylebone Cricket Club (MCC), still going strong more than 200 hundred years since its founding and the oldest cricketing organisation in the world. The MCC owns copyright to the Laws of Cricket, and remains one of the world's most active clubs, with about 300 fixtures scheduled each season.

In such an exalted place, playing on the Lord's Cricket Grounds must be heady indeed. Any young man with cricket in the blood must cherish such a memory. But not Vic: he's too down-to-earth for that.

"Yeah, I played at Lord's," Vic grins. "But I don't want to talk about it. We were *seriously* rolled over."

The last time a South African team played at Lord's was in 1965. Between 1965 and 1992 any South African representative would have been frog-marched out of the grounds. Transvaal's opponent was a World XI, a Who's Who of international cricket: New Zealand's 1991 World Cup hero Mark Greatbatch and Ken Rutherford, the English die-hard batsman Michael Atherton, the West Indies' legendary Richie Richardson and fiery pace man Joel Garner. It was a team that would have given any Test side a run for their money.

Put into bat by host captain Ian Greig, the South African Young Lions failed to raise a whimper, let alone a roar.

Vic remembers: "It was unsettling because Transvaal was the first side to tour the UK after the apartheid era. Our opening batsmen Brad White and Jimmy Cook had to wait in the change room because protesters were running onto the pitch and diving on top of the wickets. They were trying to make some sort of protest about boycotting us because we were South African. It was a horrible feeling and it made us feel very unwelcome. I thought to myself, 'What are we doing here?' White went out for five and Cook went out for 12. Wickets were falling like crazy."

When Vic went in to bat Transvaal were 52 for 5. As he stood guard at the crease he suddenly realised he had forgotten his 'box' - essential protective equipment for any batsman who doesn't want to find himself singing falsetto. The bowler, 6'6" Joel Garner, sent a ball screaming down the pitch and Vic knew he had a choice to make. He could either make his usual fearless swing at the ball and expose himself, or he could block the shot and avoid a potential ball-on-ball collision. "It was either my honour or my goolies," says Vic. "I decided to do what any wise man would have done: I protected my goolies."

The Transvaal demise was swift but painful. They posted a meagre total of 115 runs all out in just 42 of the allotted 55 overs. Vic's score was one of the highest: nine runs. He also took a catch on the boundary to dismiss the swashbuckling Greatbatch. The MCC side scored 116 for 3 in just 23.2 overs and the teams agreed to a second match. In that game Vic was the top Transvaal scorer, with 38 runs.

Vic's highest score of the tour was recorded in a two day match against county side Hertford. Vic sped to his 50 in just under an hour and sprayed the boundary with 12 fours and three sixes. He made 85 runs before he was eventually caught at deep square leg.

"We had a good tour. I learned a lot about match temperament and the stresses and pressures of living with a squad. It was also my very first time overseas; I loved travelling, loved meeting different people."

With the exception of the massacre at Lord's the young South Africans went from strength to strength. In two strenuous weeks vaal won seven matches, lost one, drew one, and had one encounter rained off. Vic notched up 165 runs on the tour, with an average of 34. It was a useful start.

At the end of the tour Eddie Barlow announced: "What we have now in Transvaal, instead of wishing and hoping for players to produce results, is a team that can deliver. We will be one hell of a side next season."

After the tour Vic and a teammate Brad White went to Greece for eight days. "It was eight days of sun, fun and dancing," Vic recalls. "We had a lovely time."

Victor returned home, now one of the best-known cricketers in Johannesburg. He was at the brink of a fine career; there were high hopes for the future of this richly talented batsman.

"When I came back from the tour of England, I had big plans," Vic recalls. "The 1992 season would be the time I made my break into the Transvaal squad."

Jimmy Cook was asked by a newspaper to identify up-and-coming hopefuls who were likely to make up a future South African team. He named Gerhardus Liebenberg (Free State); Herschelle Gibbs (Western Province), Brett Schultz (Eastern Province), Derek Crookes (Natal) and Dean Laing, Chad Grainger and Victor Vermeulen (all Transvaal). Today, eight years later, Liebenberg, Gibbs, Crookes and Schultz have all fulfilled that promise to represent their country in international cricket.

South African batsman Adam Bacher says there is no doubt that Vic and Proteas opening batsman Herschelle Gibbs would have fought each other for places in the South African Team. "I believe that he would have made the Proteas before I did."

"Yes," agrees friend and provincial cricketer Nicky Pothas, "If he hadn't had the accident Vic would have certainly been a members of the Proteas team now."

Adam continues: "Who knows, he might have even been the skipper. He was a guy who didn't let failure get on top of him. He would have been the answer to the current problem in our middle order. And Vic would never have become involved in any match-fixing, that's for sure."

As the 1992 season approached, full of promise, Vic played for Transvaal in a few friendly matches against Northerns. Then, in the warm days of the early summer, he was invited to the annual Wanderers cricket club braai.

CHAPTER 9

Going Home

With much lifting, hauling and tugging, Isabella managed to put Vic in the car. After seven months in hospital, her son was coming home. She turned the car into the driveway, got out and went inside to fetch Maggie to help her carry Vic into their Craighall Park, Johannesburg house. Vic was left alone in the car. "It was hot and I was uncomfortable," Vic recalls. "And I couldn't even roll down a window for a bit of fresh air. That's when it really hit me: life outside hospital was going to be tough."

Despite having to come to terms with his paralysis, the seven months Vic spent in hospital were relatively stress-free. "Most of the time I was spaced out on morphine, and when I wasn't friends and family were always there to distract me. And because I was in the constant care of nurses and doctors I became sheltered from the reality of my disability. I had no idea of what being a quadriplegic entailed." Coming home from the hospital changed all that.

Maggie and Isabella came out of the house and, for the first time, lifted Vic into the house. "It was like my mom was bringing home a new-born baby," Vic recalls. "But this baby was already over six foot tall."

The Vermeulen family had another baby in the house - a real one. While Vic was in hospital, Maggie Keebine, for 25 years Vic's second mom, had given birth to a son. Maggie named her newborn Victor, another Little Vic to bring light into a household darkened by the task of coping with the day-to-day reality of Vic's accident.

The hospital nurses had given Isabella a crash-course in quadriplegic care, but it was mainly through trial and error that she learned how to look after her son. Together, Vic, Maggie and Isabella discovered the best way to catheterise, how to make his stomach work, how to get him in and out of the car, how to avoid the potentially fatal risk of bedsores.

"What we learned was the value of teamwork," says Vic. "We each know what needs to be done, and we work together to get it done. If one of us slips up or forgets to do something, someone else will step in and do it, without blame or recrimination. We focus on the job at hand, and value each other's contribution. But in the beginning, each day was a struggle." This struggle was not made any easier by the fact that the family now had serious financial worries.

"We had huge medical expenses, and our medical aid had lapsed after my dad's death. My mom had a full-time job just looking after me; she couldn't go out and work. We knew times were going to be hard. I was counting on a disability pension my dad had taken out for me years before.

"When I was ten years old my parents realised that I was determined to be a professional sportsman. I was fearless and accident prone, so they worried that if anything serious happened to me - if I had an accident that disabled me in any way - I wouldn't be able to play sport. No sport; no career. So my dad decided to take out the disability pension. He approached a friend in the insurance game. His friend told my dad not to worry. He would sort it out. But when my mom tried to claim the pension she was told that I didn't have disability; I had life insurance. Children aren't eligible for disability pensions because there's a fear that parents would disable their kids deliberately in order to cash in on the pension. It turned out that we could only get a payout if I died!"

Then Bob Hodge and Natie King, friends of the Vermeulens, stepped in to help. Through the Transvaal Cricket Board they launched the Victor Vermeulen Benefit Fund. The fund was taken over by Di Featherstone, who, every year, organises a Ladies Lunch to keep the fund going, with Vic as the guest of honour.. "I always love being the only male among 400 women," Vic grins. Bob Hodge and Natie King continue to be good friends with Vic and Isabella, having become as close as family. Another good friend, Andrew Macmillan, gives Vic liquid support. When Andrew's in town, he and Vic get up to no good, just like the old days, with Andrew wheeling Vic to and from the local pub for a few pints.

Money wasn't the only worry, though. Vic had also landed in trouble with the army. After he left school Vic, like all young white men, had been conscripted to serve a year's national service in the South African Defence Force. His call up was for the July 1992 intake, but this was deferred to allow him to tour England with the Transvaal team. After the accident in November, he received another call-up ordering him to report for duty on the 31st of December. Isabella wrote to explain that her son was paralysed. The army's only response was to send another call-up.

"My mom wrote back and said that I would go to the army with pleasure, if they could make me walk. I imagined what the Sergeant Major who received the letter said: 'Corporal, ja, we've seen these pranks before. Go to Private Vermeulen's house and tell him to stop playing silly-buggers and get out of bed and come do some exercises.'"

The Craighall Park house proved too impractical for Vic and Isabella. They needed a house without so many stairs and with a double garage where a wheelchair could be easily moved around. "It takes about ten minutes to get me in and out of the car. With no garage, we had to do it in the driveway. If it rained, that would mean ten minutes in the rain. I'm already susceptible to chest infections. My mom has to cough me because I can't cough by myself. If I get a cold I could land back on the respirator."

While they searched for a suitable house, Isabella and Vic moved in with Tokkie's cousin Uncle George and George's wife Bernice. Eventually they found a small house in Randpark Ridge. They also got an electricity-powered mechanical bed to help Vic sit up and make it easier for Isabella to slide him out of the bed and into the wheelchair.

Vic's life was severely limited by his disability, but a negligent nurse ensured that it would be limited even further. "Because of my paralysis, my bladder can't contract properly to push out all the urine. I need to have a catheter, otherwise sediment stays behind in my bladder. Bacteria builds up in the urine, causing an infection that can spread to the rest of my system.

When I was first in hospital an internal pipe was inserted through my abdominal wall into my bladder. At the Pretoria hospital the doctor decided to insert a catheter through the urethra of my penis into the bladder. A thin tube goes down the penis; when it's in the bladder a ball at the end of the tube is blown up to the size of a golf ball. This is to keep the catheter from slipping out of the bladder. When the nurse was inserting the catheter, she started to blow up the ball when the pipe was still in the urethra; it hadn't reached the bladder yet. The blood vessels in my penis burst and I bled for three weeks. Finally, after a lot of nagging from my mom, the doctor discovered the nurse's error. If he hadn't, I might have bled to death.

"Because of that nurse's mistake, when I sit up my bladder doesn't drain. So I can only sit up for six or seven hours of the day. If I sit up any longer, my bladder won't drain properly and I can get bladder infections. If the urine backs up into the kidneys, causing infections there, I'm in danger of kidney failure and all its complications. So each day has to be planned very precisely. If I'm giving a talk then that day I can't go see a movie or visit a friend. If I'm going to a friend in the evening I need to spend the day in bed. We catheterise between four and five times each day. I've got a condom drain. I often tell people that I'm the only 27 year-old man in the world whose mother puts on his condom. It's a normal condom with a little gadget so a pipe can be attached.

"I had been out of hospital for a month when my mom saw that my penis and testicles were swollen. We didn't want to take any chances, so we went to the hospital. On our way a traffic cop jumped out. 'Excuse me, Ma'am,' he said in a thick Afrikaans accent, 'Do you know that you've been speeding?' 'Yes officer,' my mom replied. 'My son is ill and I'm rushing him to the hospital. My son is a quadriplegic.'

The officer took a step backwards. I could see what was going through his mind: 'Quadriplegic? Is that, er, contagious?' He waved us on.

"We got to the hospital and I was taken to the emergency unit. I was put on the bed and my pants were pulled down for the doctor to examine me. My penis was hugely swollen. 'Doc,' I said, 'take away the pain, but please - leave the swelling.' He looked at me as if I was off my head."

A few months later, a bladder infection of Vic's led to severe spasms, a high fever and a pounding headache. What he had was a condition known as Autonomic Dysreflexia (AD). AD can occur in anyone who has a severe spinal cord injury. It can be caused by a number of things. The most common are a full bladder, bladder infection, severe constipation or pressure sores. This life threatening condition causes the blood pressure to rise to potentially dangerous levels. If AD is left untreated, the body's attempt to control the blood pressure will severely decrease the heart rate. Isabella called the paramedics. While they were waiting for the paramedics, his heart stopped. Uncle George gave him mouth to mouth resuscitation. "He saved my life," Vic says. "I was rushed to Johannesburg hospital. When I woke up I saw Uncle George standing next to my bed. 'Uncle George,' I said, 'Thanks for saving my life. But don't think we've got a thing going.' Make no mistake, quadriplegia is hard. Damn hard. You can either cry about it or you can laugh. I choose to laugh."

As soon as Vic's condition was stabilised, the hospital discharged him. The following day he began to suffer more brutal spasms and pounding headaches. "I was afraid my heart was going to stop again, so we went back to the hospital. I was given tests and scans. I was being pulled and probed from about 4:00 in the morning until about three that afternoon. When it was all done I assumed I would be admitted to the hospital and the nurse would put me in bed with a drip and an antibiotic and monitor me. Instead they told me they didn't have any beds. I would have to go home."

"Mom," said Vic, "I'm sick." Isabella knows her son. He's stubborn but he never complains. If he says he's sick then it's serious. Isabella went to the nurse and pleaded. But it was in vain. "Too bad," the nurse said and marched off. Vic was taken to a private hospital and admitted to their high care unit. He stayed in the hospital for two and a half weeks.

Specialist neurologist Dr LJ 'Vic' du Plessis explains the complications - in addition to paralysis - of spinal cord injury. "There's a loss of chest muscle movement which prevents quadriplegics from coughing. So they can't cough up mucous and phlegm and are at risk of developing chest infections. Quadriplegics are also prone to breaking their bones. Lack of mobility causes osteoporosis. The calcium moves out of the bone and the bone becomes brittle and can break easily. Quadriplegics have also lost their balance and tend to fall out of their wheelchair. Because they don't feel pain, further complications can occur as a result of the unattended fracture. Due to immobility calcium moves out of the bones and into the blood, landing up in the urinary system causing kidney and bladder stones (calculi)."

Once Vic got over the initial shock of being a quadriplegic, he focussed on getting stronger and figuring out how to do the activities in life that he enjoyed. He knew that this would give his life some semblance of order and control. "Life is full of big and small changes and sooner or later we need to face them. I suppose I could have given up and said, 'I haven't got use of my arms and legs so what do you expect?'"

But that's not what Vic is about. He didn't give up, he decided to bounce back and make the most of his life within the limitations of being a quadriplegic. Facing a life-change as severe as quadriplegia is devastating, but he worked on ways to beat the blues and take the edge off the pain. Maintaining a positive attitude and not giving up allowed Vic to make small gains, little victories, each day. These bolstered his confidence and sense of self-worth. "It's important to realise that quadriplegics fight tremendous battles every single day. The more I mastered, the more empowered I became. I made myself a victor rather than a victim.

"After I was discharged from hospital I realised that it was important to exercise. Three times a week - an hour a time - I would go to physiotherapy. I went religiously because I wanted to stop my body from further breakdown, I wanted to keep my muscles in shape for the day there's a cure, and I was determined to get any movement I could back and become as functional as possible."

Vic worked hard at physiotherapy, but his injury had been so severe virtually no movement was regained below his shoulders. "There wasn't any functional movement," explains Jenny Michaeli, Vic's occupational therapist. "Vic was going to do very little by himself. Nothing came back despite the fact that he worked hard. And nobody worked as hard as he did.

"We concentrated on his neck and shoulders because it was all we had to work with. I used to make him push his wheelchair using his shoulders. I strapped his arms on the wheels and, using only shoulder power, he would push himself up and down the corridor. A physiotherapist would put him over a big barrel and she would put his hands down on the ground. This was to improve his sense of balance. We had to strengthen up his neck so that he could use it to control his posture.

"I decided he must go in the swimming pool. We are weightless in water so it's easier to exercise quadriplegics in the pool. Because the water wasn't very deep and Vic is so tall we put him on his knees. With me holding him from the back and the physiotherapist guiding him at the front, he walked on his knees through the water. One day we were walking through the water and I lost my grip. Vic fell headfirst into the physiotherapist's boobs. When we finally managed to get him up, he looked up with a cheeky grin and said: 'Now, that's a *nice* way to drown.' Anybody else who nearly drowned would have freaked out. Not Vic.

"He's an amazing person. Each session I had with Vic was the highlight of my day. He may not be a Springbok on the field but he sure is a Springbok in his attitude. He taught me about perseverance. I've never felt sorry for him. It upsets me that such a terrible accident should happen to a guy like him, but I don't see him as simply a guy in a wheelchair. I see him for what he is: a very, very able person."

CHAPTER *10*

A Day in the Life

Vic dreams of one day walking again, when the cure for spinal cord injury is finally found. He keeps his muscles as limber as possible, not only to maintain his health now, but so that they are ready to go if that cure is found. He doesn't live in false hope, he just hasn't given up hope. But in another way, Vic is still walking: at night, when he sleeps.

"When I dream I'm always walking. Once I dreamt that I was in a wheelchair and there was a girl drowning. I jumped up out of the wheelchair to save her. Sometimes, for a split second after waking up, I've forgotten that I'm a quadriplegic. I start thinking about my plans for the day and then, bang, it hits me: I'm trapped in a concrete body. There is no escaping it.

"Our routine is a finely tuned operation that actually begins the night before. At 10 p.m. Maggie turns me. This takes about 20 minutes. The reason for having to turn is to prevent bedsores. People with spinal-cord injuries don't just sit in a wheelchair. Our bodies deteriorate all the time. One of the most serious things that can happen is skin breakdown. The average person constantly shifts his weight a little so no area of the skin gets constant pressure on it. At night you turn 64 times without knowing it. I'm not able to do that. If I'm not turned, the constant pressure of my body on the bed will starve areas of tissue of oxygen. The tissue dies, infection sets in and bedsores develop.

"Bedsores are far more serious than people think. I've seen sores you can put your fist in. People have died from them. If I get a red mark on my skin it's already too late. Once there is a mark on the outside, there is damage inside: tissue is already dying. If we see a mark we put ice on it for five minutes, no more, no less. The cold draws the blood to the area of the bedsore, restoring oxygen and preventing more damage. In the eight years I've been a quadriplegic I haven't had a single bedsore. That really is a tremendous achievement. It's a tribute to my mom and to Maggie; it shows how well they care for me.

"After I've been turned at 10 p.m., I'm strapped to the bed. This is in case I have spasms in the night; it stops me falling off the bed. Remember, I've had spasms so bad I once fell right off the bed and hit my head on the floor. I was lying on my stomach. I couldn't lift my neck: I thought I'd broken it again. Luckily my mom is always within earshot. She came rushing in and helped me back onto the bed.

"It's very comforting to know that she's always near me if I need her, but there's a price to pay: my privacy. Getting used to having no space of my own, and no independence, has been one of the hardest adjustments I've had to make. Since I was a little boy I've been fiercely independent; having to depend on other people all the time is difficult for me. And it's humiliating to be handled like a baby - to need somebody to wash me, dress me, deal with my body waste and do absolutely everything else for me.

"After I've been strapped to the bed I sleep until the alarm rings at 3 am. That's when my mom comes in to turn me for the second time in the night. While I'm turned, we catheterise. My stomach works three times a week, we call it 'bollie', an Afrikaans euphemism we learned from the nurses at the hospital. On bollie nights, after the 3 am catheterising, my mom inserts a suppository. The alarm is set for 4:30 a.m. - that's when my stomach works. But if it doesn't work, my mom has to remove the stools manually. At 4:45 a.m. we are finally finished and once again we settle down to sleep. If I'm lucky I fall asleep; otherwise I lie awake trying not to think about how thirsty I am. I don't want to call my mom, she's been up twice already."

The alarm rings again at 7:30 a.m. The top of Vic's bed is elevated for him to adapt to the drop in blood pressure which occurs in quaduplegues with change to the upright posture. Then the rest of the early-morning routine: in goes the breakfast, off go the pyjamas, on goes the lathering cream for a shave, in goes the toothbrush, sponge bath, catheterise, turn, wash Vic's hair, dress him for the day.

"What I go through each morning is commonly known as a Shit, Shave & Shampoo. After being dressed, I'm taken off the bed and my clothes are pulled straight. I'm positioned comfortably in the wheelchair. My mom combs my hair. This routine takes precise planning and team work. Everybody knows exactly what their job is, when to do it and why. If we don't work together, we won't win together."

"Nothing can be postponed until tomorrow. If I don't catheterise and if I don't turn I'm going to be in trouble. That's why we don't have holidays. What we do at our home, we've got to do on holiday, but it's more difficult because we don't have the electric bed and the home comforts.

"Although there is one holiday I'll never forget. My mom, Maggie and I went with Uncle George and his wife to the Kruger National Park. We had seen elephants, giraffes and rhinos, but we hadn't seen any of the big cats. We were driving around lion country when one of the tyres punctured. Understandably Uncle George was reluctant to stop and change the tyre when lions could be lurking nearby. After a while it was clear that we had to change the tyre or the entire wheel would be ruined and then we would have broken down completely. My uncle jumped out, leaving the car door open. I had a vision of a lion leaping in and pulling me out. I wouldn't be able to do anything. My mom jumped out to help. In a flash the wheelchair was out, the spare tyre was out; the flat wheel was in the boot, the wheelchair was back in the boot, bolts were fastened and the spare tyre was on. It was so quick that the next day I expected to receive an offer from Ferrari to employ a red-headed woman and a balding man in their pits."

Getting Vic in and out of the car was also difficult and initially Isabella was unable to do it by herself. They would arrive home and she would run around the complex trying to find somebody to help. One day there wasn't anybody to help. Vic suggested they sit in the car until somebody came along. "No," said Isabella. "I'll take you out by myself." "Mom," replied Vic patiently, "You can't do it." But Isabella is stubborn, just like Vic. She did it. "Vic couldn't believe it," recalls Isabella. "For hours and hours he blabbered on about how wonderful I was." Isabella developed a knack for transferring Vic into the car; it's a precisely choreographed performance that's amazing to witness. She has a little board which she slips under Vic's buttocks. Then she grabs him by his pants, puts him over her shoulder, puts her foot in the car and slides him across the board and into the car. Voila.

Vic just spent the day in Durban. He flew there in the morning and flew back later that afternoon. I asked him to count how many times he was put in the wheelchair. "Jon-Jon," he phones that evening, "16. I was in and out of the wheelchair 16 times." In the morning he was transferred from his bed to the wheelchair; wheelchair to car; out of the car at the airport and into the wheelchair; up the hydraulic lift and out of the wheelchair and into a seat on the plane. If he's travelling in a small plane he's taken from the wheelchair into a 'slip chair' and onto the plane. From the plane he's transferred to the wheelchair and down the hydraulic lift at the airport in Durban. From the wheelchair into the car. Vic was then transferred into the wheel-chair at the place where he was due to deliver a motivational lecture. Then it was out of the wheelchair and into the car. Out of the car and into the wheelchair to the restaurant for lunch. From the restaurant into the car. Out the car and into the wheelchair at the airport. Up the hydraulic lift and into the plane. Down the hydraulic lift and into the wheelchair back in Johannesburg. From the airport and into the car. Then from the car it's into the wheelchair into the home and then out of the wheelchair and into bed. "Every single time my mom carried me by herself," says Vic proudly. "Thank goodness I've put her on steroids," he chuckles.

Isabella and Vic were slowly discovering how difficult the ordinary could be for a quadriplegic. Like their combi experience. "Soon after

I left hospital we bought a combi because we thought it would be easier to travel around in. It wasn't. We needed two ramps to wheel the chair into the combi. My mom needed help because the wheelchair is heavy and I didn't have balance to duck under the door. In the combi I'd be facing backwards. I couldn't bend my head to see the people sitting in the car next to us. All I could see was the white lines on the road flash by. We had the roof extended so there was more room for me. All we needed was music and the combi would have resembled an ice-cream van.

"One day we arrived at the hospital and we wanted to drive through the gates into the parking. My mom asked the security guard if we would fit through the gate. 'No problem,' he said. My mom asked him if he was sure. 'Yes,' he answered, 'Go, go, go." We got stuck. My mom jumped out of the combi. The security guard could see the anger in this redheaded woman's eyes and took off. He ran up the road and never came back. I think he could see my mom was going to give him a slap around the gums. A Portuguese man on the scene suggested, 'You letta the tyres down?' but my mom didn't think this was such a good idea. Instead they stood on the bumper and bounced the combi and we came unstuck. The next day my mom sold the combi."

Part of the routine Vic and Isabella were gradually establishing was taking in to account when and where his stomach would work. This made for some bizarrely funny incidents.

"One day I had to go to physiotherapy, but my stomach hadn't worked properly the night before. I was dreading my session because I just knew that as soon as it began my stomach would decide to work. We arrived and the therapist put me up on the stand-up frame, equipment that's designed to help my blood circulate. Sure enough, as I stood up I felt my stomach wanted to work. Most quadriplegics can't tell when their stomach is working, but I can, for some unknown reason. I told my mom that she was going to have to take me down and, after all the effort of getting me out of the bed and into the car, we would have to go home. The therapist suggested we use the room in the back to clean up and then continue. So Maggie went to the car to fetch the extra bag of clothes we carry just in case something like that does happen. Unfortunately, although we had spare tracksuit pants, we didn't have underpants. I couldn't just put on a pair of tracksuit pants. I was afraid that when I was in the stand-up frame, Percy would point at the physiotherapists walking by. My mom had a bodysuit that buttons up in the front. She said she would clip on her bodysuit and she'd put her black lace panties on me. 'No ways,' I said to her, 'you're not doing that to me. It's bad enough being paralysed, but I'm not being a quadriplegic in drag! I'm not putting your black panties on, mom. Do you hear me?'

Maggie was also outraged: 'No, no, ma'am you can't do it! No, no! Listen to Vic, you can't put black panties on him.' But my mom's stubborn. She wouldn't be persuaded and on went the black lace panties.' I warned her that she wasn't to tell a soul. I couldn't wait to get home. I couldn't even feel the black panties but I felt weird: What have I come to? I'm wearing my own mother's black lace panties! It felt so bizarre, even though nobody else knew.

While Vic jokes about his disability, he's doing it to make other people feel more comfortable. He understands that faced with his condition the best thing for him and for others is to laugh. "Humour is what makes it bearable," he says. "I don't think it trivialises what I'm going through. It helps everyone cope with the situation."

Vic's friend Adam Bacher recalls another example of Vic's rich sense of the absurd. At Adam's wedding reception he overheard Vic in conversation with Adam's uncle, United Cricket Board president Dr Ali Bacher, one of the most powerful men in South African cricket.

"Doc, when am I getting my call up?" Vic said.

"Call up for what?" Dr Bacher was confused.

"For the South African cricket side, of course. As you know, there's been a lot of talk about the quota system for cricket. Ensuring that the previously disadvantaged are represented in our national squad.

"Yes?"

"And the new Equity Bill has outlawed any discrimination against the disabled."

"Of course."

"Well, I think that makes me eligible for the side. Anyway, I'm a brilliant night watchman. Just put me in front of the wickets and they'll never get me out. Have you ever heard of the wheel before wicket rule?

"No."

"Exactly. And I don't need leg pads even if they bring on all the fast bowlers of the world. It's not like I'm going to feel it if the ball hits me. All I need is a helmet. I've been to the south of Johannesburg, I've learnt how to head butt. I'm sure I can get you a few byes off my head."

On another occasion, two women from a religious sect notorious for its members' very intrusive attempts to convert the general public, came to visit Vic in order to convert him. They also became the victims of Vic's active sense of humour. "We were having a lovely chat and my mom decided to make coffee and tea. While she was in the kitchen I told these women that I was so happy they were there. I don't think too many people have said that to these women. They normally kick them out the door. Their eyes went wide like saucers. I asked them to try and keep my mom in the room because she boozes and then, when she's drunk, she beats me. They were horrified. When my mom came back in the room there was no longer a friendly atmosphere. They looked at her as if she was Satan. They drank their coffee and left. I told my mom what I had done and she was outraged. I explained that I was just having a little bit of fun; keeping myself amused. A week or two later these women came back and again my mom went to the kitchen to make coffee. I said to them, 'Remember what I told you about my mom last week.' They nodded. 'Well, I lied.' This time they looked at me as if I was Satan. They came back for

85

quite a while and we remained friends. But they no longer try to convert me."

Vic knows it's not only the disability that makes life difficult; it's all the things that come with it: inaccessible transport and buildings, high cost of essential medical equipment, unfair policies, and, worst of all, people's thoughtlessness. I learn this the day Vic, Isabella and I decide to go and see a movie at a Johannesburg mall. We pull up next to a blonde girl in a sports car. Vic starts to flirt. He nods, winks and bobs his head up and down. She flicks her blonde hair back. If she were any cooler she would be in the fridge. She flashes just a hint of a smile. She's clearly interested. "Vic," Isabella reprimands her son. Then Vic looks at his mom and the two burst out laughing.

We arrive at the mall and discover that there is no spare bay in the parking reserved for people with disabilities. "It's very frustrating," Vic says. "People can be so unbelievably thoughtless."

Disabled parking bays are provided for two very important reasons, although many able-bodied people seem to think they're just a way of reserving prime parking space just for them. Firstly, they are close to the entrance of the mall to allow the disabled - in a wheel-chair, on crutches or using a walking frame - easier access to the mall. The bays are also wider than normal so that the car door can open wide and the wheelchair can be placed next to the door to make it easier for the disabled person to go in and out of the car.

With all the disabled parking taken, Isabella has to manoeuvre into a bay in the regular parking area. She parks half way out of the bay to allow enough space to take Vic out of the car. She's blocking the way; a man in a hurry, hoots and shakes his fist. Vic shrugs his shoulders. "What's our alternative?"

When we get to the entrance of the shopping centre we see a perfectly fit young woman climb into a car parked in the disabled zone. "Excuse me," says Vic, "Why have you parked in a disabled parking bay?" The woman looks embarrassed. "Oh," she splutters, "my mother's a paraplegic."

"So where's your mother?" The woman is flustered. She's not used to being confronted. "She's in Durban," she manages to stammer before speeding off.

"I don't think it's because people are horrible that they are inconsiderate," Vic explains. "I think people just don't think. They have no idea how complicated, how very difficult, everyday life is for the disabled. They don't realise that the little things they do, small acts of selfishness like taking a disabled parking bay, can complicate a quadriplegic's life even more. Maybe if they were exposed to what we do behind the scenes - getting up at 3:00 am, my mom blowing my nose because I can't, catheterising four times a day - then perhaps they would be less selfish.

"Even my friends and family don't always seem to appreciate how difficult my life is. When I'm at a braai with friends and I'm enjoying myself, the last thing I want to do is go home to catheterise. My friends may beg me to stay, but I have no choice. I have to go."

There is no direct wheelchair access to the cinema complex in the shopping centre, only escalators. So we have to use the goods lift, which is tucked away back in the service area. To get there we have to go down a concrete corridor littered with discarded rubbish from the shops. We're greeted by the stench of rotten cabbages and trash. "We're lucky," says Vic. "Sometimes the corridor is so full of rubbish that we can't even go through." The lift is working - sometimes it isn't - but the lights aren't. When the doors close on us, it's pitch black inside.

At the cinema Isabella waits in the queue to buy the movie tickets and Vic and I get something to drink. The coffee shop waiter asks me what I want. Then, with a nod in Vic's direction, he looks at me and asks: "What can I get him?" I'm about to retort, "Vic's disabled, he's not brain dead," but Vic has already stepped in. A fly is hovering nearby and Vic turns to the waiter and says, "Nobody must tell me flies are stupid." The waiter looks puzzled. Vic continues: "Because there will be 50 able-bodied people in a room and the fly will come and sit on the quadriplegic who can't swat it away." The waiter laughs. Vic's made another friend.

87

We go back and I notice that people stare at Vic. Two teenagers even giggle. Vic smiles and greets every stare with a cheerful hello. His self-confidence is remarkable.

There is only one cinema that claims to be wheelchair accessible. It isn't. The management has simply taken out two chairs in the back row and pronounced it accessible, but the space isn't wide enough to actually fit in a wheelchair. Vic has to sit in the aisle. It's dark and a young girl carrying a coke and popcorn doesn't see Vic and bumps into the wheelchair. She spills her coke and popcorn all over him. A man walks in a few minutes after the movie starts. He stands in front of Vic while he waits for his eyes to adjust to the darkness.

On the way out we see a man alight from the car that he's just parked in the disabled parking bay. "Do you know this parking is for the disabled?" Vic asks him. "I'll park where I like," the man mutters darkly before storming off. "People's attitude is so frustrating," Vic sighs again.

Disability creates potholes in the highway of life. When Vic came out of hospital he felt as if he was stranded in the emergency lane while all his friends were tearing down the highway: getting married, having children and advancing in their careers. "It's difficult for me because I'm a twenty-seven year-old man who still lives at home and can't even control his bowels without the help of his mother. But I think that difficulty has just brought out the best in the things I've had all along: my mind, my heart, my attitude to life. I've been incredibly unlucky, but I've beaten that bad luck by taking it on with a positive attitude. Nothing beats a positive attitude. I may be paralysed, but like everyone else facing difficulties in life, I've still got a choice. I could have decided that I was just a victim and I could do nothing about it, but I chose to get on with my life, with my relationships, my work, with all the things that make this life we have such a gift. I know it's likely that I'll be paralysed for the rest of my life, and I want to enjoy it. Or there could be a cure tomorrow. The thing is, even if that cure does come, I don't want to think that I've wasted all my life just waiting for it."

CHAPTER 11

Min Dae

When Victor Vermeulen and I first met, I was just a journalist doing another job; he was just another interesting person whose story I had to draw out and get down on paper. Then, gradually, over weeks spent with him, his mother and Maggie at his home, we became friends. As Vic told me about his life, the image of the quadriplegic in a hospital bed slowly disappeared from my mind, to be replaced with that of a bright, strong young man with immense physical and emotional courage. Vic was a great sportsman, dedicated to his cricket. But more than that, he's a great guy with a generous heart and a wicked sense of humour: a good friend. And as I became more emotionally involved, I started to be haunted, like all those who care about Vic, by thoughts of what might have been.

There's no doubt Vic would have made it in to the South African national cricket squad. The future was bright. Some people wonder if, with his natural leadership, his positive attitude and ability to inspire others, he might even have become captain.

I remember one afternoon at Vic's house when we were watching the live broadcast of the King Commission into cricket match fixing. There on the screen was South African cricket captain Hansie Cronje, crying as he told the world about money he'd received from bookies during his stint as skipper. Some of us lose opportunities in life through terrible accident, I thought. Others just throw them away.

What ifs are melancholy questions to ask, but with Vic you can't avoid them. What if he'd never gone to that cricket braai? What if it had rained that night, making swimming out of the question? What if those girls had joined Vic and his friends ten minutes later, when they were already in the pool? The thing is, these questions are useless, and Vic knows it.

Vic's philosophy is that happiness is always right there, in our grasp. But so many of us don't reach for it, because they've convinced themselves that they can only be happy if things were somehow different. If they were richer, if they were thinner, smarter, younger. What ifs aren't only useless, they can be destructive.

But there's another 'what if' that isn't such a bad question: What if they find a cure for spinal cord injury?

Vic is 6'3" tall and I'm 5'6", yet when I look at him, I have to look down: in a wheelchair, on his bed. What are the chances that one day Vic will walk into the room and I'll look up to say, "Hi there big guy"?

There seems to be no agreement anywhere as to when, and if, there will be a cure for spinal cord injury. Some say clinical trials are only two years away, others say twenty years. And then there are those that throw up their hands and say, "Not in our lifetime..."

This is mainly because the spinal cord is such an incredibly complex piece of bodily equipment. Basically, the spinal cord is the brain's second-in-command: anything the brain wants to get done in the body has to go through the spinal cord. Together, the brain and the spinal cord make up the body's central nervous system, or CNS. This is the most important, and the busiest, of the body's systems and organs. Other systems concentrate on only one job: the circulatory system, for example, just supplies oxygen to the rest of the body via the heart and lungs. Easy enough. But the circulatory system couldn't do this without instructions from the CNS, and while the CNS is controlling circulation it's also telling everything else in the body what to do. The CNS is the ultimate multi-tasker: it controls all movement in the body, both voluntary (all the movements we consciously make, like walking, scratching, turning the pages of this book) and involuntary (all the movements the body gets done without our specific instructions, like the flexing of our chest muscles required for deep breathing and coughing, the blinking of our eyes, the expansion and contraction of our bladders). And while it's busy with that, it's also regulating our sleep, monitoring our thirst and hunger, controlling our balance and spatial orientation. Each day, from when you jump out of bed in the morning to that craving for hot chocolate before you sleep, thank your central nervous system. And spare a thought for those whose CNS has been crippled by accident; those whose brains work fine, send all the important messages, but whose hotline to the rest of the body, their spinal cord, has become disconnected.

Because it's so important, so central, to the work of the body, the CNS is the most well-protected system. The brain is safely encased in the hard bone of the skull; the spinal cord inside the hollow bones of the vertebrae. But this protection is a double-edged sword. If any injury occurs to the bony armour protecting the brain and spinal cord, the bone itself can cause damage. Skull fractures and spinal breaks can send shards of sharp bone into the vulnerable nervous tissue. And if that tissue is in any way traumatised, bruised or bisected, blood rushes to the site of injury. The resultant swelling is held back by the protective bone. The pressure exerted by bruised and swollen nerve tissue straining unrelieved against the inside of the hard vertebrae is one of the causes of permanent damage to the spinal cord.

Like any complex organisation, the body has worked out some good risk analysis. The organs and systems most vulnerable to damage are also the most capable of self-healing and regeneration. The skin, for example, exposed as it is to all the dangers of the outside world, can heal itself remarkably well, as any of us who remember the pride of showing off our scars to the other ten-year-olds in the playground can testify. But the spinal cord, locked away inside layers of skin, fat, muscle, and bone, is the safest of all the body's systems. So the body has taken out no insurance; if there's damage, there's nothing the body can do about it. Because it's so specialised, and because it's so well protected, nerve tissue in the spinal cord does not regenerate. Once the spinal cord has been severed, it won't grow back.

For this reason, spinal cord injury, or SCI, has always been seen as a hopeless case. Once you're paralysed, that's it. You're a paraplegic - paralysed from the waist down - or a quadriplegic - paralysed from the neck down - for the rest of your life. But few people realise that this attitude is in fact an improvement on the view previous generations had of SCI. In the last fifty years, we have already made enormous strides in treating the symptoms of the injury. Before the second world war, if you broke your neck or your back, you were dead. Most deaths occurred from complications that today are easily controlled: bladder infections, respiratory infections, respiratory failure and pressure sores. A lot of spinal cord injuries are the results of gunshot wounds or similar violence: just the sort of thing to happen in war. For this reason, a lot of soldiers returned from the Vietnam war in wheelchairs, and the American Veterans Administration is closely involved in the search for a cure to SCI. But soldiers who suffered the same injuries in the First World War, a war fifty years earlier that devastated an entire generation of young men, returned not in wheel-chairs but in coffins.

The twentieth century has already seen enormous advances in our understanding and treatment of spinal cord injury. From a mortality rate of more than 90 percent, we have advanced to a stage where over 90 percent of those with SCI survive to live out a normal life span. Surgical advances allow the injured spinal cord to be stabilised, eliminating the need for prolonged hospitalisation. Medication can now improve the amount of movement and sensation a person can get back after injury; certain kinds of surgery are also improving function. Drugs also help eliminate pain and control spasticity.

Those who say there is no hope after SCI are wrong: enormous progress has already been made in the twentieth century. The twenty-first century will surely see scientists and the disabled community impelling the search further, until the cure is found.

The first major milestone in that search turned the accepted wisdom of SCI on its head. In 1988 Martin Schwab of the University of

Zurich discovered that regrowing spinal nerves wasn't so impossible after all. He identified two types of protein in the body that actively prevent the regeneration of these neurons. Although spinal nerves don't have any nerve growth factor - they can't instruct themselves to regrow after an injury, like the skin - they can be artificially stimulated to do so. What Schwab discovered was that all previous attempts to get this growth on the go had failed not because spinal nerve cells can never, ever regenerate but because the body, through the two proteins he identified, was actively preventing this regrowth.

This was a major breakthrough: science had for years dismissed any possibility of a cure by declaring, "Spinal nerves just don't grow back." Schwab developed an antibody to block function these inhibitory proteins, and in tests on animals was able to stimulate regrowth of nerve cells in the spinal cord. But Schwab and his colleagues have not yet been able to make a satisfactory form of this antibody for use on humans.

Another important development didn't happen in a medical lab, it happened on a horse. Or rather, it happened when film star Christopher Reeve fell off his horse and broke his neck. From Superman he went to a C2 quadriplegic - the most severe SCI disability there is. He has no movement below the neck, and can't breathe on his own; he's permanently connected to a respirator. Christopher Reeve's accident was an enormous tragedy for the actor, his friends and his family, but his misfortune has become a boon to the global SCI community.

The world was horrified to see this handsome, well-loved actor, a man in his prime, reduced to the most severe form of quadriplegia there is. Accolades and encouragement poured in from all over; US president Bill Clinton phoned Reeve in hospital. All of a sudden, the world became aware of the devastation spinal cord injury can wreak on a person's life. Although initially reluctant to do so, Reeve has used his high-profile image to become the poster boy (his words) to raise awareness of quality of life issues for those with SCI, and to campaign for greater efforts in the search for a cure.

Through a merger with the American Paralysis Association, Reeve set up the Christopher Reeve Paralysis Foundation, or CRPF, the largest organisation in the United States devoted to SCI issues. The mission of the CRPF is to support research into effective treatments for paralysis caused by SCI, and ultimately to find a cure. Apart from an international individual research grant program, the Foundation also supports the CRPF Research Consortium on Spinal Cord Injury, a network of scientists in eight laboratories who pool their wide-ranging expertise and work co-operatively to solve the complex challenges of repairing the injured spinal cord. All of these efforts are donor-funded. Christopher Reeve is also an activist in the struggle to get the governments of the world to take the possibility of a cure more seriously, and to actively support research efforts. The main problem, as Reeve sees it, in the search for a cure is not the intractable complexity of the spinal cord but, rather, funding. It is disheartening for any paralysed person to hear leading researchers say, "If we raise 300 million dollars, we can find a cure for paralysis in 5 years instead of 15." As Reeve says, "Most disabled people would agree with me that it is very difficult to cope psychologically with the stark reality that our future depends mostly on money."

For this reason, Reeve uses his profile to campaign for greater government funding into SCI Research. The world may be increasingly conscious of the need for wheelchair access, but Christopher Reeve can get into places no other quadriplegic can. He has spoken in front of the US Democratic Party National Convention, the National Press Club, the National Organisation on Disability, and has taken his mission to Washington, where he testified before the USA Senate Appropriations Subcommittee responsible for the funding of health issues. Thanks to Reeve, there is hope that the paralysed community of the world will no longer have to suffer the paralysed attitude able-bodied governments and organisations seem to have towards them, and their future.

But funding of research into SCI has become controversial, because of another important breakthrough in the search for a cure. In the late 1980s, it was reported that paralysed cats had improved function after stem cells were transplanted into their spinal cord. Stem cells are undifferentiated cells that, once transplanted to the site of injury, can survive, grow and differentiate properly, repairing some of the damage. This is a very promising therapy, but a controversial one. Stem cells are in fact fetal cells; they are taken from embryos or foetuses that are the result of abortion. There is an ethical debate as to whether this research should continue, and in 1995 the US government voted that no research involving the use of stem cells was to be funded by the Federal government.

But stem cell research is by no means the only initiative in the search for a cure. In January 2000, progress in genetic research allowed Martin Schwab and his colleagues at the University of Zurich to identify the human gene for the protein which inhibits spinal nerve regrowth. This discovery holds promise for the development of an antibiotic to the protein that can be used on humans.

Another approach is remarkably simple: developing vaccines to fight the growth-inhibiting proteins. Sam David and his colleagues at the Montreal Institute of Neurology inoculated mice with spinal cord extracts, three weeks before spinal cord transection. Half of these mice were able to walk again after their spinal cords regenerated. The regrowth was not complete, but in some of them over 75 percent of the severed nerves grew back. Obviously, the success rate here was not the best, and many technical problems remain, not the least of which is that the vaccination was required before the injury.

Scientists have also looked elsewhere in the body to see if there is any place where nerves do regenerate. They found it in the nose. The olfactory nerve, which carries smell messages to the brain, has a unique ability to heal and regrow. This is made possible by special cells known as olfactory ensheathing glia, or OEG. By transplanting these cells to the spinal cord, it would be possible for the OEG to work their magic on spinal nerves. Some successes have been

95

reported from Spain in using this procedure on rats, but trials on people are yet to begin.

Nerve growth factors, known as neurotrophins, could also be used to stimulate the regrowth and survival of spinal nerves. These growth factors can be used alone or in combination with other therapies, such as antibodies to inhibitory proteins and stem cell transplants, to get the spinal cord growing. A study at the University of New York has shown that neurotrophins can also get the nerves of the spinal cord to ignore growth inhibitors. And a report from Harvard Medical School identifies a substance called isonine as a powerful stimulant to spinal nerve regrowth.

All of these therapies have made progress in the year 2000. It is clear that the pace of the search for a cure is accelerating. And there are many more attempts underway, many more laboratories in the world that are approaching the problems of paralysis from a variety of different perspectives. Predictions made fifteen years ago about when a cure would be found could not have anticipated any of these advances; predictions we make today cannot take into account what might be discovered in fifteen years time, or in five, or tomorrow.

Christopher Reeve has drawn some criticism for his optimism; many believe it is wrong to encourage false hope. Predictions are not an exact science; no-one can really say when, if ever, the cure will be found. Some believe that it just won't happen; that the cure, if it is found, is many decades away and will in the best case only be partial. Others, like Reeve, maintain that it is all just a matter of money, and that medical science, having worked remarkable, seemingly impossible miracles time and time again in the past, must surely also get this one right, and soon.

But where does this debate get the person in the wheelchair? It's a question of hope.

People with spinal cord injury have one of the highest suicide rates of any group, any population, in the world. As Wise Young, a medical doctor, spinal cord injured himself and active in the SCI community, puts it: "Most people do not commit suicide because they have had too much hope and were disappointed. Rather, they commit suicide because they have been deprived of hope. Pessimism has long been a self-perpetuating prophecy in spinal cord injury."

There is a phrase many of us remember from when our fathers, our friends and brothers, or we ourselves were conscripts in the South African army. The phrase is min dae. Conscripted against their will at the age of 18, forced to put up with all kinds of unpleasantness for two years, soldiers with six months or so left of their period of service would end letters home with a hopeful, "min dae." It's an Afrikaans phrase, meaning literally "few days"; it's come to mean "not long now; there's light at the end of this tunnel."

I'm at Vic's place again, and we're talking about the cure. Martin Brown, a quadriplegic friend of Vic's, has just heard of a new break-through in stem cell research. He faxes the report through, and I have a read. The Christopher Reeve Paralysis Foundation has announced that a laboratory in its Research Consortium, headed by Dr Ira Black, has developed the first successful procedure to convert cultured bone marrow stem cells into nerve cells. This will allow for an abundant source of cells to treat spinal cord injury. It's not the cure, but it's another good step towards it. It's exciting, and Vic and I discuss it. Before I knew Vic, I didn't even know how to spell quadriplegic; now, advances in the cure for his condition seem to be in the news every day. They were there all along; I just hadn't noticed them. Then I notice something Martin had got his aide to scrawl at the bottom of the report.
"Lots of love. MIN DAE!"

CHAPTER 12

Mother's Pride

Victor is on stage, giving a motivational talk at a conference. The theme of the conference is heroes. Sitting next to him is his mother, Isabella. Vic talks about his cricket career, his accident, his struggle with his quadriplegia. The audience is still, silently enthralled by the man on the stage. Some are in tears. Every twenty minutes or so, Vic pauses, inclining his head slightly. His mother gives him a sip of water from a glass and he continues. The flow of his talk is barely broken; Isabella understands the needs of her son so well it just take that slight movement of his head for her to know he needs some water. Vic and Isabella are as close as any mother and son can be: not only is she now his arms and legs, she's also his nurse and his best friend. And she, as Vic will tell anyone, is his hero.

Vic's talk comes to an end, and he rounds it off with a song. "I would like to play this song as a tribute to my mom," he tells the audience. "The woman who has been a bundle of support, care and love." Bette Midler's song *The Wind Beneath My Wings* is pumped out through the speakers:

So I was the one with all the glory,
while you were the one with all the strain.
A beautiful face without a name for so long.
A beautiful smile to hide the pain.

Did you ever know that you're my hero,
and everything I would like to be?
I can fly higher than an eagle,
for you are the wind beneath my wings.

While the words of the song echo through the hall, photos flash on the wall. There's rosy-cheeked Vic as a toddler, Vic with Isabella and Tokkie, Vic playing cricket, Vic dressed up to go to his matric dance, Vic signing autographs, Vic in hospital, and Vic in a wheelchair with Isabella behind him. The last photograph is especially poignant. It's a photograph which has captured the Vermeulens' fighting spirit; a celebration of triumph, and of a mother's pride.

Isabella and Vic. Vic and Isabella. Their relationship is unique. Isabella knows Vic better than any mother knows her son. There are no secrets between them simply because there can't be. It's true that together they laugh and have fun, lots of it, but there are also those moments when the never-ending circles of enduring and those "what might have been" frustrations threaten to swallow them up. Remarkably these moments are very infrequent. In the months I spent with the Vermeulens I witnessed only one minor incident. It was a misunderstanding over a temperamental fax machine, which developed only into an irritable debate about what grey button to press. Then Vic cracked a joke about "safe faxing" and the two were giggling together like schoolkids.

"We can't afford to sulk with each other," Vic later tells me. "It wouldn't work."

Anybody who has ever spent time with Isabella and Vic knows how she dishes out generous doses of affection to her son; kissing him and fussing over him, telling him endless jokes and stories, and just being there; always being there. "If it wasn't for my mom it would have been so much harder," says Vic. "Knowing that my mom has her eye on me and that she will not leave makes things okay. No amount of money can buy me that security."

100

It wasn't only Vic's life that changed forever on November 5 1992. Isabella has lost as much freedom as her son. Their lives have merged. "If somebody had told me that my son would be paralysed and I would have to care for him," she says, "I would have said, 'No way. I don't want anything to do with it.'" But Isabella underestimated herself. "I saw him in hospital and I remember thinking, here is the little baby I gave birth to, that I nurtured, and that I love. Now he's lying on the bed, fighting for his life. Vic's a fighter; he fought an enormous battle, against all odds, to live. I couldn't let him down after that."

"When I saw Vic on that hospital bed I remember thinking of a doll that I had when I was a young girl. The doll's arms and legs were connected inside the body with a piece of elastic. One day the elastic broke and the doll's hands and legs fell off. Here is a big, strapping 6'3" good-looking man who can't move a thing. Vic's elastic had been broken. I couldn't believe that something like that had happened, but there was no time to think about it. I had to take the reins and carry on. I had no choice. Vic is my son and he's worth fighting for. There was no time to be selfish or to feel sorry for myself. Vic is my life.

"I knew nothing about nursing, but I knew I would get through it. I have a fighting instinct, and Vic believed in me. He was so certain that I could cope; his positive attitude gave me strength. I thought that if he could face this tragedy with brave acceptance then so could I.

"We are with each other 24 hours a day. Whatever he does, I do too: bathing, washing his hair, cleaning his ears, blowing his nose, coughing him, exercising his fingers, arms and legs, removing his stools, catheterising. When I buried my husband I thought I had lost the best friend I had ever had in the world, that I would never again know friendship like that. I was wrong. I've got just such a good friend in my son. The more we are together, the closer we become. And we have a rich and interesting life. We really are best friends."

Isabella Vermeulen radiates positive energy and an obvious enjoyment of life. She is always cheerful. Yet her life, since she was a small baby, has been repeatedly punctuated by profound tragedy and loss. When she was two weeks old her mother died. She went on to survive a grave illness, the brutal murder of her husband and the complete paralysis of her son. To know why she succeeds you have to understand one thing about Isabella: she fights back.

Isabella credits her grandmother with giving her a fighting spirit. "She gave me inner strength. I was born on a farm in Wilgespruit in 1938. Two weeks later my mother died. I was the baby in a family of four. My eldest sister was nine, my other sister was five and my brother was two. We were going to be shipped out to various family members when my grandmother put her foot down. She wanted to look after us, all of us, as a family. My father retreated to his farm in the bushveld. My mother's death really affected him. I never really knew my father: we were virtually strangers to each other. My gran became the person I loved, the person I felt safe with.

"My gran was 60 years old, a widow, and running a farm by herself. Her only help was from her 16-year-old son. When my sisters went to high school my dad got a little flat in town for them, and my brother went to stay with my dad in the bushveld. I stayed behind with my gran and my uncle. They both doted on me. It was a blissful time.

"When I was a teenager my gran suffered from bronchitis, which got worse with each passing year. Finally, when I was 25, she became gravely ill. One night I slept in the bed with her in case she needed me. During the night she started to splutter. I thought she was choking because of the bronchitis. I lifted her, patted her back and put her down on the pillow. When I turned to see how she was doing, she gave a little gasp. It was her last breath.

After her death the farm didn't feel like home any more. I moved to town and opened a hairdressing salon. And I started to have some fun.

I wasn't looking for some magical kind of romance, but it wasn't long before it found me. At a party one night, I noticed a very handsome man. I found out that this was Henry Vermeulen, whose friends called him Tokkie. He cut a dashing figure. Even before I spoke to him

I knew that this man would be important to me. I stood around with a glass of beer, being witty and full of nonsense, just like Vic is today. Tokkie thought I was drunk because I was playing the fool. But I've never been drunk in my life. I was just holding the beer for effect, to appear sophisticated. I hate beer! He asked me to dance - he was a very good dancer. We just clicked.

"About a month later I went to a party with a boyfriend. Tokkie was there with a partner. During the night Tokkie and I danced together while his partner and my partner sat talking. At the end of the evening Tokkie and I said goodbye, and he told me he wanted one last dance with his 'girlfriend' before he left. Then he took my hand and danced with me. With a little wink, he slipped his telephone number in my hand. He was so smooth, but in those days girls didn't run after boys. He found out where I worked and phoned me there. Because we danced so well together he suggested that I join him, his cousin George and George's wife Bernice for cha-cha classes. It sounded like fun. When Tokkie came to pick me up he told me that George and Bernice couldn't make it, but suggested we go to the drive-in instead.

"We had been going out for about six years when late one night Tokkie was driving home and someone drove into the back of him. He arrived home at 2 o'clock in the morning, woke me up and said: 'Do you want to marry me or not? If we were married I wouldn't have been on the road at this time of the morning.' I said yes.

"On our wedding day, a friend was driving me to the church when I asked him to stop and park under a tree. I was having second thoughts. I told him I wasn't sure if I should get married. I loved Tokkie, but I asked my friend, how do you know when you are ready? 'Because you'll never find a better man than Tokkie,' my friend replied. I thought of Tokkie - the charming man with the infectious laugh - and I knew he was right.

"During the ceremony the priest produced a rosebud from his pocket, which he had picked that day. He said to us, 'Henry and Isabella, look at this rose. See all the tiny thorns on the stem. You will

103

have thorny days in your marriage: when you do, look at this rosebud to remind yourself of how beautiful it is, and remember what you promised each other here today.' When my husband died, I put the rosebud in the coffin with him."

One of the thorny days was when a doctor told Isabella she would be unable to have children. But three years after the wedding, she miraculously fell pregnant.

"When I brought Vic home, Tokkie was over the moon. Those were happy, happy times. When I held Vic, I remember thinking I would give my life to save this little boy. That I would protect him always. I know that there is nothing I can do to make him walk again, but I also know I can help make his life worth living, as he has made mine. I see Vic in his pram; Vic curled in his bed; Vic wiping his dog's bottom; I see Vic as a rosy-cheeked boy with a naughty grin who approached life with a unique flair. I see a bright, achieving child who was always up to some mischief. I see a caring and concerned boy who, like his father, always wanted to help people. I see Vic as a resolute cricket player determined and talented, but always having fun. I also see Vic with his dad. He idolised his father; theirs was a very special relationship. And now, I see the brave, strong man Vic has become. I know Tokkie would have been proud of him.

"Only God knows what strengths Vic has had to call upon in this situation. The weird thing is that I am not angry. Far from it. In fact, I'm grateful. Vic may be unable to fix himself a glass of water, but I am grateful for his clear eyes, his sense of humour and the open relationship we have. I love him."

The tape falls silent. My wife and I have been listening to the recording of Isabella's memories made earlier in the day, and my wife is in tears. Then Vic's voice comes on, and we can clearly hear the grin in it.

"I have a cool mom," he says.

CHAPTER *13*

Take a Look at the Life

A few years after his accident a friend asked Vic if he would speak at his church youth group. Vic agreed. In front of the roomful of teenagers he smiled, joked and without a hint of bitterness chatted about his life. He told them that he, sitting in his wheelchair, was a good example of the curve balls life can throw at all of us. We have no control over how that ball is thrown; how fast it's going, or how it will bounce. But we can control how we bat at it. However devastating our misfortune, we haven't lost our ability to choose. The most important choices we can make are how we decide to deal with the curve balls of life: we can let our circumstances control us, or we can control our circumstances.

Just before midnight on November 5 1992, as Vic told the kids before him, he was young, happy and healthy, standing around, talking and playing the fool with his mates. Only a few minutes later he was completely paralysed and near death. And yet years later here he was, in a wheelchair for sure, but still happy and healthy, a mature man with an enjoyment of life much larger than many who can walk. The group of youngsters hung on to every word, but Vic wasn't to know that among them was a boy whose life he had just saved.

Two years later Vic was giving a talk to the Johannesburg Junior Mayor Council where he was approached by a young man. A matric pupil, the teenager was in uniform, a Prefect's badge on his blazer.

"Vic," he said, "I need to thank you. You probably don't remember me, but two years ago you spoke at our youth group. I have to tell you: I'd decided to commit suicide. But after listening to your talk, I chose to turn my life around. You turned your bad fortune into something positive. I realised how stupid I'd been, that with all the opportunities I had, I was still feeling sorry for myself. It was time to take responsibility. I woke up the next morning and as tribute to you I joined the cricket team. I'm not the best in the side - in fact I think I'm probably the worst - but I really enjoy it. And I made prefect. I don't take my life for granted any more."

If you've ever thought quadriplegics were sad, forgettable cases sitting drooling in wheelchairs with nothing to do, think again. Vic Vermeulen has been on a speedboat, he's looped through the sky in an aerobatics display, and he's put a hospital bed on the back of the bakkie to go trekking through a game reserve looking for animals. He's done a lot more than many of us, and with the odds against him stacked much higher. He had his accident when he was just a boy, nineteen years old with only a widowed, jobless mother to support him. Plug that into any statistical computer and you'll come out with tragedy and sadness. Then take a look at the life of Vic Vermeulen.

"It was just chance that sent me into that pool, at that angle, at that time, to break my neck. But there were signs all through my life that I would have some serious challenge to overcome. I've broken my back before - remember, my vertebrae were smashed in water polo. And my parents named me Victor. A victor is not someone who gets all of life's advantages and then succeeds. A victor is someone who has to struggle against something, something fighting against him, his happiness, his life, even, and still succeed.

"But to be a victor doesn't mean you engage in a single, do-or-die fight. Sometimes victory takes small steps.

"As I lay in hospital I knew I had to rise to the challenge, or be nothing. After I was discharged, I knew I would have to adapt to life as a quadriplegic a day at a time. It's been hard, no doubt about that. I won't pretend that sometimes I struggled to find the light in this dark situation.

"I thought I had my life all planned out, that I'd make a name for myself as an international cricketer. I never doubted that dream; I never thought I wouldn't make it. Obviously, being confined to this wheelchair is not something I would have chosen. But with all the radical changes the accident made to my life and my dreams, I had to do the best I could on the new road life had mapped out of me."

At first, Vic tried to fight his disability, struggling to overcome his paralysis. But after three determined years of physiotherapy and rehabilitation, he finally realised that he wasn't going to get anything back. "It felt like I was going to cricket practice, always facing in the nets but never going out to play in the middle, in front of a crowd. It was time to focus my energies on doing something else. I started painting, using my mouth to hold the brush. I did art at school, but I never thought I was talented. I only did it because in the other classes I had to listen to a teacher drone on and on, but in the art class we could talk and listen to music.

"I learned that although it's important to set high goals, it's also vital to appreciate each small success. I focused all my attention on completing a painting; the painting became a metaphor for my new life. If you've ever tried to draw a picture holding a pencil or a paint-brush in your mouth, you'll understand that it is impossible to view your work properly. Sometimes we can't see the big picture. I was determined to persevere and not allow my limited vision to stand in my way. This was the first goal I set myself - a single objective that gave me a renewed sense of purpose and made me feel worthwhile. And I achieved that goal because I was passionate about achieving it. Intense desire, it seems, not only creates its own opportunities but also its own talents.

"In creating my paintings I learnt three important principles for constructive living. Firstly, although I found it frustrating to paint while not being able to see the whole canvas properly, I refused to allow that frustration to make me quit. I had set myself a goal and I wanted to experience the feeling of accomplishment that comes with success. Secondly, I learnt how to plan steps to achieve my goal. Thirdly, and perhaps most importantly, I never attempted to deny my feelings of fear, frustration and anxiety. By admitting to them, I decided to use them to my advantage to achieve my goal. I gave my first painting to my mom; I wanted to thank her for still believing in me. Painting gave me a new lease in life, because I was creating something, I was being useful and I was doing it by myself.

"People heard about my paintings and a couple of fundraising evenings were organised to auction them off. I painted two fish eagles, flowers, a fisherman, portraits of cricket players, a kudu, springbok, and Table Mountain. It was amazing for my self-confidence. Unfortunately, squinting at a canvas only the length of a brush away was hurting my eyes. So I had to give it up. I didn't want to risk ruining my eyes because that would limit my life even further.

"Then Peter Stringer, a friend, suggested I coach cricket to up-and-coming players. This did even more to bolster my confidence. In the beginning the boys were a bit nervous of this coach in a wheelchair, but once they discovered that I knew what I was talking about, they accepted me. Initially I sat behind the nets so I could speak to the batsmen and tell them what to do. Then I sat on the side of the nets, facing square, so if I looked left I could see the batsman, and if I looked right I could see the bowler. But it was difficult. Try to explain something without using your hands to get the point across. I learnt quickly how to be precise with my words so the boys could understand my instructions. Move your left foot a little bit forward. Okay, bend your right leg a little bit. Okay, that back elbow, tuck that in next to your side so the bat can come through straight.

I coached at the Wanderers and then I was approached by Helpmekaar High School to coach one of their senior sides. I also coached four or five youngsters privately. I had a purpose; a reason to wake up in the morning. I witnessed their progress and it gave me immense pleasure when one of them would attribute a good performance to the advice that I had given. I went with the team to watch games and the captain would ask me about field settings and strategy. I loved it. It gave me a taste of the camaraderie of my own cricket days. Helpmekaar had a very good season and a lot of guys did well in the trials for Nuffield week."

Then came the motivation. Vic's good friend Andrew Kramer relates how three years ago he was sitting at a family meal telling everybody about Vic and his remarkable attitude to life when one of his mom's friends said that it sounded like Vic had a personality for motivational speaking. "I spoke to Vic and made an appointment at the Voice Clinic for him. Helping to push him in that direction is one of the things in my life that I'm most proud of. He'll turn your thought process around. His energy is electric. Being in a wheelchair is incidental; it just makes his message more powerful," says Andrew.

"My coach at the Voice Clinic was a tremendous man called Vaughn," says Vic. "Although at first I was a little disappointed. 'Gee,' I thought, 'there are so many beautiful women teaching here, and I've got to be put with a guy.' I soon realised how lucky I actually was. Vaughn was a Godsend. He taught me how to project my voice and he gave me incredible confidence. I went for about three months.

My last session was on a Friday. I said goodbye to Vaughn. He wished me luck for Monday - the day I was due to give my speech as the last part of the three-month voice-training programme. Vaughn told me that of all the people he has trained, he believed I was the most suited to motivational speaking. He said that to motivate his other clients he would rave on about gutsy Victor Vermeulen; the man who never says he can't. That weekend, Vaughn had a stroke and died. It was as if he waited to help me so I could go and do my talks and help other people.

"I was then invited to speak on 702 Talk Radio. I mentioned that I would like to get into motivational speaking. A woman from the Multirand Forum was listening. She invited me to apply to be a speaker at an insurance conference. I had to address a panel of ten people who were choosing the conference speakers. My mom asked if the venue was wheelchair accessible, they said yes, but it wasn't. We had to go up a steep ramp, then up a few steps and into lift and then another lift and then up an escalator, but the escalator wasn't wide enough for the wheelchair. So we went down the lifts back into the parking garage to search for the goods lift. I was ready to turn around. It's a good thing I didn't. I gave a ten minute presentation and one of the men on the panel stood up and said, 'That's the best speech I've ever heard.' I was chosen for the conference.

"At the conference I was given a standing ovation at the end of my speech. A lot of people were crying. Felicia Mabuza-Suttle, the talkshow host, was the MC of the conference. She said I touched so many people's hearts. She asked if I wanted to go onto her show to touch the hearts of millions more. She was crying. 'Felicia,' I said, 'I'll come on your show with pleasure as long as you stop mocking my disability.' She was taken aback. Then I explained that I can't touch. From crying, she burst out laughing. I went on to the Felicia show and cellphone network MTN offered to put me on a retainer to talk once a month at different schools.

Things just fell into place, and I found myself on the speaking circuit. I met former president Nelson Mandela. Like a lot of people, he made the mistake of offering a handshake when we met. I told him I couldn't shake his hand, not because I'm a racist, but because I'm totally paralysed. He laughed and then told me he would pray for a full recovery.

"To travel the country making motivational speeches is what makes my life exciting and challenging. But it's still a challenge, very day. At any moment I may have to cancel a talk because I could get a bladder or kidney infection. And as a person in a wheelchair, there are always logistical problems to overcome.

"Sometimes, before I speak I think about my life. What happened to my vision to play cricket? Well, it went wrong. The things I had been dreaming about, planning for, working toward since I was three years old were no longer possible. But so what? I make friends and I have wonderful experiences, which no one can ever take away from me. I'm just as successful now as I was before my accident. Whenever one door closes, another opens. If I hadn't broken my neck, I wouldn't have become a motivational speaker. I would have touched lives, but only as entertainment, as a sportsman people could watch on the cricket pitch. Now, I not only touch people's lives, I can change them for the better. Through my accident, I have been allowed to make a far more positive impact on the world. My message is that what is easily seen is a small percentage of what is possible."

"When everything is going your way it's easy to be passionate about life. Anyone can steer a boat when the sea is calm; the challenge is to steer it in stormy seas. A sign of success is being able to be enthusiastic no matter how difficult the situation that you find yourself in. What would happen if you became paralysed? Think about it. Would you be devastated, unable to continue living, unable to feel the same passion for life? I became paralysed and I'm back up there with the best again, with a new vision that's mine. Troubles, difficulties, adversity: expect these, because they are an inevitable part of life, but never stop dreaming. Be like a postage stamp: stick to something until you get there.

"Many people have told me I am such an inspiration to them, but I don't really know why, and it makes me feel a bit embarrassed. I'm just an ordinary person who happened to break his neck. All I've done is find a way to handle my situation that works for me."